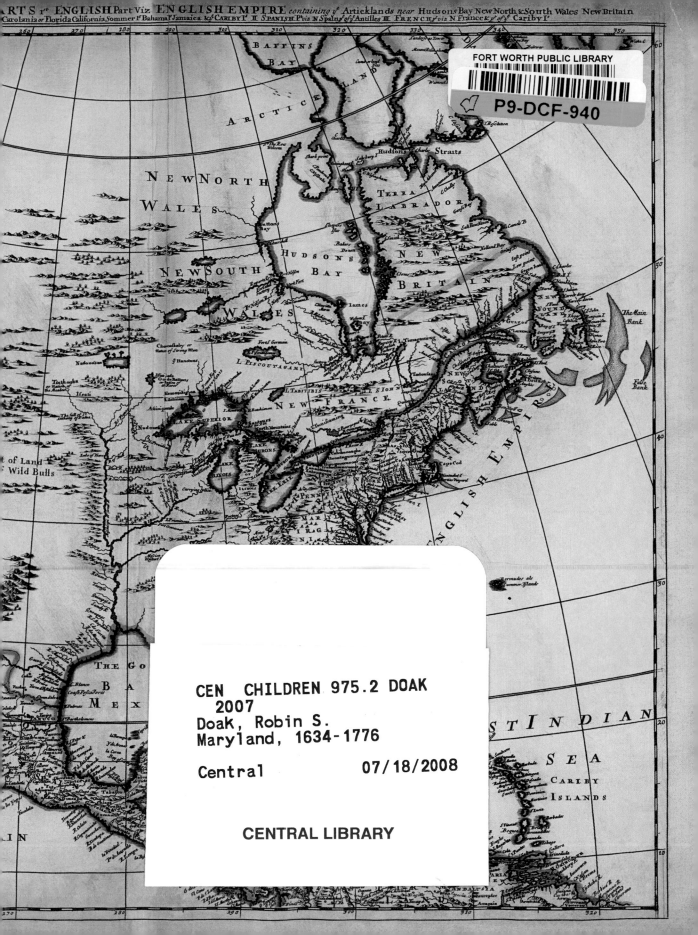

· VOICES ·
from
COLONIAL AMERICA

MARYLAND

1634 — 1776

ROBIN DOAK

WITH

JAMES D. RICE, PH.D., CONSULTANT

NATIONAL GEOGRAPHIC

WASHINGTON, D.C.

John M. Fahey, Jr., *President and Chief Executive Officer*
Gilbert M. Grosvenor, *Chairman of the Board*
Nina D. Hoffman, *Executive Vice President; President, Book Publishing Group*

STAFF FOR THIS BOOK

Nancy Laties Feresten, *Vice President, Editor-in-Chief of Children's Books*
Amy Shields, *Executive Editor, Children's Books*
Suzanne Patrick Fonda, *Project Editor*
Robert D. Johnston, Ph.D., *Associate Professor and Director, Teaching of History Program University of Illinois at Chicago, Series Editor*
Bea Jackson, *Director of Illustration and Design, Children's Books*
Jean Cantu, *Illustrations Specialist*
Carl Mehler, *Director of Maps*
Justin Morrill, *The M Factory, Inc., Map Research, Design, and Production*
Rebecca Baines, *Editorial Assistant*
Jennifer Thornton, *Managing Editor*
Connie D. Binder, *Indexer*
R. Gary Colbert, *Production Director*
Lewis R. Bassford, *Production Manager*
Nicole Elliott and Maryclare Tracy, *Manufacturing Managers*

Voices from Colonial Maryland was prepared by
CREATIVE MEDIA APPLICATIONS, INC.

Robin Doak, *Writer*
Fabia Wargin Design, Inc., *Design and Production*
Susan Madoff, *Editor*
Laurie Lieb, *Copyeditor*
Cynthia Joyce, *Image Researcher*

Body text is set in Deepdene, sidebars are Caslon 337 Oldstyle, and display text is Cochin Archaic Bold.

LIBRARY OF CONGRESS CATALOGING-IN-PUBLICATION DATA
Doak, Robin S. (Robin Santos), 1963–
  Maryland, 1634–1776 / by Robin Doak.
    p. cm. — (Voices from colonial America)
  ISBN: 978-1-4263-0143-8 (trade)
  ISBN: 978-1-4263-0144-5 (library)
  1. Maryland—History—Colonial period, ca. 1600–1775—Juvenile literature. I. Title.
  F184.D63 2007
  975.2'02—dc22
                                    2007027886

Printed in the United States

CONTENTS

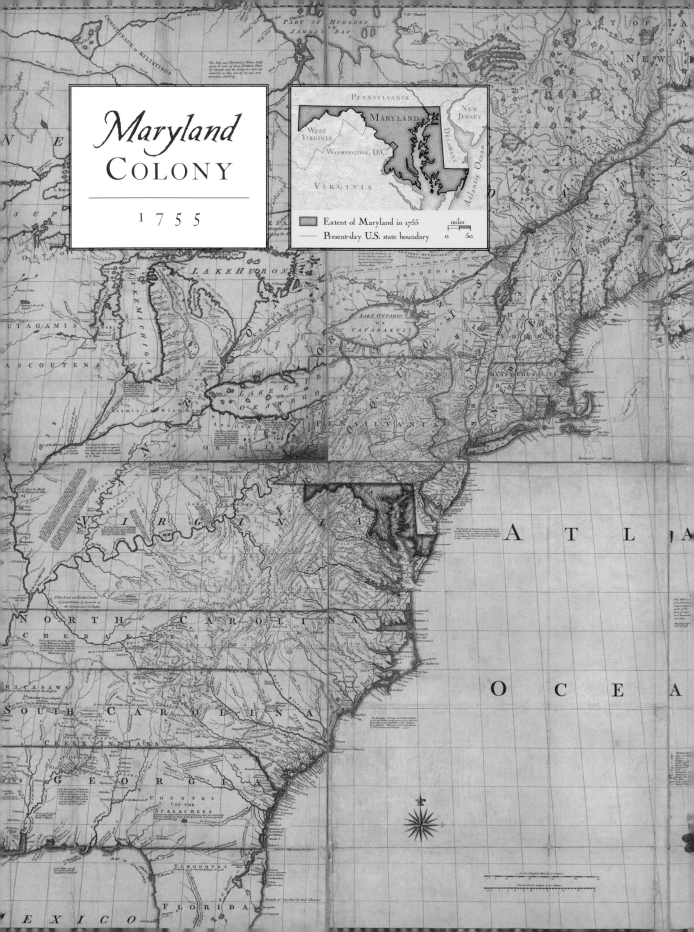

Maryland
COLONY

1755

Extent of Maryland in 1755

Present-day U.S. state boundary

miles

0   50

INTRODUCTION

by

James D. Rice, Ph.D.

The Maryland State House in Annapolis, completed in 1779, is the oldest
state capitol building still used for government business. The city of
Annapolis briefly served as our nation's capital city in 1783.

If present-day residents of Maryland could go back to colonial times, they would hardly recognize the place. Roads
were little more than paths, and almost everyone lived in
scattered settlements along the rivers. Although there was
some trade with the Algonquian Indians, most people made
their living toiling in the fields, growing mainly tobacco.

OPPOSITE: This historical map, created by John Mitchell in 1755, has been
colorized for this book to emphasize the boundaries of the Maryland colony.
The inset map shows the state's present-day boundaries for comparison.

It would be difficult, at first glance, for a 21st-century visitor to the colonial era to see how it paved the way for life in modern Maryland.

And yet, it did. Many tobacco workers in the 17th century were desperately poor Englishmen who agreed to work for several years in exchange for passage to America, for food and shelter during their servitude, and for a small package of "freedom dues" upon their release. The tidewater region of eastern Maryland quickly developed as more and more land was cleared for tobacco farming. After about 1680, European servants were increasingly replaced by enslaved Africans who had been torn from their homes—a great tragedy that has as its legacies both America's history of troubled racial relations and contributions to cultural diversity.

Tin glazed plates with this design were known as Merryman plates. First manufactured around 1680, the plates featured verse emphasizing the kindness and generosity that women brought to a home. Excavations at sites in St. Marys City, Maryland's colonial capital, have unearthed shards of these dishes.

Maryland was owned and ruled by a single English family, the Calverts. The Calverts were Catholics at a time when England was militantly Protestant, and they wanted Maryland to be a refuge for persecuted English Catholics. Most of their colonists, however, were Protestants. This led to so many disputes over religion that Maryland's government adopted a policy of religious toleration, which has since become one of the most important ideals in American politics.

In the 18th century, the western part of the colony filled up with colonists after 1730 due to an influx of Germans and Scots-Irish immigrants who moved from neighboring Pennsylvania. By 1750, the western Maryland town of Frederick had become the colony's largest urban settlement. Meanwhile, well-off planters in older settlements near Chesapeake Bay moved to cities such as Annapolis and Baltimore, which soon outgrew Frederick. Maryland colonists felt proud to be British, especially when Britain gained control of all French territory in mainland North America after the French and Indian War (1754–1763). Disputes over the taxes imposed by the Crown to pay for the British victory over France, however, soon led to the American Revolution. During the Revolution, many leading Patriots came from Maryland—as did a number of Loyalists. After the Revolution, Maryland showed its centrality to the new republic by ceding land for the creation of the nation's capital city, Washington, D.C.

I am delighted to serve as the consultant for *Voices from Colonial America: Maryland*. Maryland—as is true of the United States as a whole—has never ceased to be a place where people regularly confront issues of religious and cultural diversity and the challenge of living up to their own high ideals of civic life.

CHAPTER ONE

Native Americans and Spaniards

BEGINNING IN 1542, *European explorers venture into the Maryland region. Later, Bartholomew Gilbert, John Smith, and other English adventurers come into the area.*

During the colonial period, Maryland and Virginia were the two Chesapeake colonies, named for Chesapeake Bay. In the early 1600s, Maryland was part of the Virginia colony. After Maryland became a separate colony, it and Virginia continued to share similar economies. In the early days, they also faced many of the same challenges. However, Maryland developed its own unique character throughout the 1600s and 1700s.

OPPOSITE: Native Americans watch from the shore as English captain John Smith arrives in Chesapeake Bay. England was the last of the European powers to explore the area.

BEFORE THE ENGLISH

More than a century before English settlers built homes in the region now known as Maryland, adventurers from other European countries explored the Chesapeake area. In 1524, Italian sailor and merchant Giovanni da Verrazano sailed along the eastern coast of North America. Exploring for the king of France, Verrazano traveled from present-day South Carolina all the way to what is now Rhode Island. Although the Italian captain completely missed the mouth of Chesapeake Bay, he did make anchor along Maryland's Eastern Shore. His voyage gave France its claim to North America.

In 1561, Pedro Menéndez de Avilés, a Spanish explorer, became the first European to explore Chesapeake Bay. Menéndez named the bay Baya de Santa Maria (the Spanish name for Chesapeake Bay), or St. Mary's Bay. He returned to the area in 1568. Twenty years later, Spaniard Vicente Gonzales explored the bay up to its northernmost shore. These expeditions gave Spain a claim to the region, too.

THE FIRST PEOPLE

Native Americans lived in the Chesapeake Bay area long before Europeans ever set foot on the land. The first people to live in what is now Maryland may have arrived as early as 12,000 years ago. These people were nomadic hunter-gatherers. They moved from place to place to take advantage of the best times for fishing and hunting.

By the early 1600s, a number of native groups lived in the region. Most of the tribes were of the Algonquian family, meaning that they shared the Algonquian language and similar customs. The most important groups on the Eastern Shore were the Choptank and the Nanticoke, although many other tribes also lived there. The Nanticoke were allied with the fierce, powerful Powhatan of Virginia. Like other native people in the area, the Nanticoke were both farmers and hunters. In the summer and fall, tribe members lived in settled villages along the coast.

As in other Algonquian nations, each Choptank and Nanticoke village was led by a *werowance*, or chief. The title was passed down from the eldest brother in a family to the youngest. If all the brothers in that generation had died, the title was passed to the oldest sister or her eldest son. The werowances had the power to wage war and to forge agreements with other Native American groups. They had many advisers who helped them

Artist John White painted this 1585 portrait of an Algonquian Indian of the Maryland region.

make important decisions. The people of a village took care of its werowance by offering tributes of food and other goods.

Villages were made up of round, domed houses called *yeahawkans*. Each yeahawkan was made by bending a frame of branches into a domed shape. The branches were tied into place with pieces of rawhide or vines. The dome-shaped frame was then covered with tree bark or mats made of reeds. Inside, in the middle of the dirt floor, the Indians built a hearth for a fire. A hole in the top of the yea-hawkan allowed smoke to escape.

The Nanticoke, like other area tribes, grew the "three sister" crops—corn, squash, and beans. They also gathered nuts, berries, and edible wild plants to supplement their diet. And like other area tribes, the Nanticoke grew tobacco. When English colonists arrived in Virginia, local tribes taught them how to grow and smoke this "weed." The Virginia colonists then passed this information along to the new arrivals in Maryland.

The Nanticoke and other Chesapeake tribes used dugout canoes to travel on the big bay and explore the many rivers and streams that fed into it. The Chesapeake itself was an important source of food for the Nanticoke and other native peoples. They caught fish and eels and col-lected clams, oysters, and crabs to eat. Oyster and clam shells were made into spoons, bowls, and wampum. Wampum—purple and white beads made from shells—was used as money when trading with other tribes.

In the winter, the Nanticoke would move away from the coastline into the interior. During the winter and early spring, the men hunted for deer, elk, turkeys, squirrels, rabbit, ducks, and geese, using bows and arrows, spears, and traps. The skin, fur, and bones of the animals were used to make clothing and tools. In June, when game ran low, the Indians moved back to their villages.

On the Western Shore lived the Piscataway, the Yaocomaco, the Pawtuxant, the Nacotchtank, and many other tribes. The Piscataway, who made their home on Piscataway Creek, were the most powerful of these groups. Their leader, known as the *tayac*, served as the chief of many tribes in the region. Unlike the Nanticoke, the Piscataway lived in the same village year-round. They farmed, hunted, and fished for food.

One of the few non-Algonquian tribes in the area was the Susquehannock. This Iroquoian tribe lived along the Susquehanna River, which flows into Chesapeake Bay. They were known as fierce fighters who often raided Algonquian villages to the south.

In the early 1600s, Englishman John Smith became the first European to meet the fearsome Susquehannock, or "people of the muddy river." The Powhatan had warned Smith that these hostile Indians to the north were cannibals. Smith described the Susquehannock as tall, intimidating giants who spoke in deep voices and carried iron hatchets and knives.

John Smith maps Chesapeake Bay in 1608 in a shallop, an open boat
powered by oars and sails, designed to maneuver easily in shallow waters.
Early English explorers used these small, heavy boats in the New World in
order to meet and trade with Native Americans living along the coastline.
The boats were often built in pieces in England, loaded onto the larger
ships crossing the ocean, and assembled in North America.

THE ENGLISH IN THE CHESAPEAKE

England believed that it had a longstanding claim to North
America. In 1498, John Cabot, an Italian explorer sailing
for England, became the first European explorer to visit
Newfoundland in present-day Canada. He was the first
European to lay claim to the North American mainland.

Nearly 100 years later, England attempted to found its
first colony in North America. Roanoke, Virginia, settled
in 1587, was a failure, and its colonists disappeared. In
1603, English captain Bartholomew Gilbert made anchor
off the Chesapeake's Eastern Shore. He and some of his

crew went ashore, where they were killed by natives. The same year, English explorer Samuel Mace may have visited the Chesapeake.

Virginia's first European settlement, Jamestown, was founded in 1607. Jamestown was also the first permanent English settlement in North America. In June 1608, John Smith and 15 colonists began the first in-depth explorations of Chesapeake Bay, then considered the eastern limit of the Virginia colony.

Smith was amazed by the bounty of the Chesapeake region. He described the fish in the bay as *"so thicke with their heads above the water that for want of nets . . . we attempted to catch them with a frying pan, but we found it a bade instrument to catch fish with."* During the voyage, Smith nearly died from an infection caused when a stingray drove its poisonous, spiked tail more than an inch into his arm.

ONE BIG ESTUARY

IN THE EARLY 1600S, JOHN SMITH HAD NO IDEA THAT HE WAS exploring the largest estuary in what would become the United States. An estuary is a partially enclosed body of water where fresh water from a river or stream mixes with salty ocean water. Chesapeake Bay receives fresh water from more than 50 rivers, streams, and other smaller waterways. Estuaries are important ecosystems where many different types of animal and plant life thrive.

Smith returned to Jamestown, then almost immediately headed out on a second expedition. This time, the explorer met some of Maryland's native people, including the Nanticoke and Susquehannock. Although the Nanticoke at first greeted Smith with a volley of arrows, they later became friendlier. Smith traded with the Nanticoke people, offering them trinkets for food, water, and animal furs.

Smith did not venture far into the interior of the region. He said, *"All the Country is overgrown with trees."* Smith was the first to describe the two arms of the bay as the "Eastern Shore" and the "Western Shore," names that are still used today. Smith found that many freshwater rivers and streams emptied their waters into the salty bay.

This map, found in a collection of books titled *Narratives of Washington and the Chesapeake Bay* which includes first-person accounts of colonial life and histories of the earliest towns and cities, shows the boundaries of Virginia (labeled) and Maryland which is illustrated as forested territory.

Commemorating
SMITH'S EXPLORATION

IN DECEMBER 2006, THE CAPTAIN JOHN SMITH CHESAPEAKE
National Historic Trail was created. The water trail follows
Smith's exploration of the bay during his two trips in 1608
and 1609. Beginning and ending in Jamestown, Virginia, the
trail covers about 1,500 miles (2,400 km) of waterways. The
first part of the trail follows Smith's route along the Eastern
Shore, then crosses the bay to Baltimore. It then winds
southward along the Western Shore and up the Potomac
River to Washington, D.C. The second leg of the trail travels
up the bay to the mouth of the Susquehanna River, with
stops along the Patuxent and Rappahannock Rivers.

In all, Smith spent nine weeks exploring the
Chesapeake region. Afterward, he created a "Mappe of
Virginia" that provided future explorers and settlers with
the first drawings of the Chesapeake shoreline. The map
was the most accurate and complete of its time and included
rivers and Indian villages. Maryland's first settlers would
rely heavily on Smith's map when they arrived in later years.

John Smith's map, although not completely accurate,
continues to be used today. Modern-day archaeologists use
Smith's placement of native villages to
choose dig sites. Many of the villages disappeared shortly after Smith mapped them
due to European settlement. ▓

archaeologist—a scientist
who studies the past by
uncovering items people
used in their daily lives

CHAPTER TWO

The English Settle In

THE ROMAN CATHOLIC CALVERT FAMILY *is given owner-ship of land that will become Maryland. After settling St. Marys City, the new owners must contend with English settlers and natives who are already living in the region.*

I n the late 1620s, an English nobleman named George Calvert, the first Lord Baltimore, began planning a settlement in the northern section of the Virginia colony. In 1629, Lord Baltimore asked Charles I of England to grant him a charter for a siz-able chunk of land there.

Before he settled on the Chesapeake area, Lord Baltimore had favored a colony farther north. In 1620, he

OPPOSITE: Leonard Calvert (in black hat with sword) barters with Native Americans for land in southern Maryland.

was granted land on the island of Newfoundland. Lord Baltimore named this settlement Avalon, after a mythical island connected with the legendary King Arthur. He abandoned the project after an unsuccessful attempt at founding a colony there. The fishing business that Baltimore hoped would support the new colony was not a success, and disease and harsh weather killed many of the first settlers.

Calvert was a Roman Catholic, and one of his goals was to create a colony where Catholics and other persecuted religious groups would be allowed to worship freely. At this time, anti-Catholic feeling ran high in England. Catholics had been persecuted in England since the reign of King Henry VIII, who had split from the church in order to divorce his first wife. And because two of England's traditional enemies—France and Spain—were Catholic countries, Catholics in England were viewed as disloyal and untrustworthy. As a result, Catholics were prevented from holding important government offices.

When members of the Virginia colony learned of Calvert's request, they were unhappy. They didn't want anyone encroaching upon their territory—especially a group of Roman Catholics. Although members of the Virginia Company tried to prevent Calvert from receiving a charter, they failed. In June 1632, the king awarded the Calvert family its grant. Unfortunately, George Calvert did not live to enjoy his moment of triumph. He had died two months earlier. Instead, the charter was given to his son Cecilius.

The charter granted to Cecilius, the second Lord Baltimore, a new colony around Chesapeake Bay. The land was named Terra Maria, or Maryland. Under the terms of the new charter, Cecilius (and, later, his heirs) had considerable powers as owner of the land. Lord Baltimore and his appointed officials could grant portions of it and govern as they saw fit. He also had the right to tax the landowners in his colony. In return, he was required to pay the king two Indian arrowheads each year.

Cecilius Calvert, the second Lord Baltimore, to whom the charter for Maryland was granted

Cecilius quickly set to work putting together an expedition to settle his colony. He convinced several Catholic gentlemen to settle in and help fund the new colony by giving them large chunks of land. Calvert intended these gentlemen to be the colony's aristocracy, or upper class. About a hundred Protestants were also recruited to settle in the colony in order to fulfill his idea of a community of religious tolerance.

Cecilius chose his younger brother Leonard to head the expedition. Once in the new colony, Leonard would serve as Maryland's first governor. Realizing that anti-Catholic sentiment would be strong in neighboring Virginia, Cecilius warned his brother to *"cause all Acts of the Romane Catholique Religion to be done as privately as may be."*

Cecilius raised funds to purchase two small ships, the *Ark* and the *Dove*. The ships set sail from London in mid-October 1633, stopping briefly at the Isle of Wight, a small island in the English Channel. There, two priests and their servants were secretly brought aboard. By November 22, the ships were once again under sail and on their way to Maryland. The departure was planned so that the settlers would arrive in time to plant spring crops.

One of the priests on the expedition was Father Andrew White. White kept a careful journal of the expedition, called *A Brief Relation of the Voyage unto Maryland.* At the start of the trip, a fierce storm separated the two ships. The winds were so strong and wild, wrote White, that *"this amazed the stoutest hearts."* The rest of the trip was uneventful, however, and in February 1634, the settlers arrived in Virginia.

Father Andrew White, a member of the first expedition to settle Maryland, conducts a Catholic mass for the settlers upon their arrival in the New World.

IN THE CHESAPEAKE

Although Cecilius had warned his brother Leonard to avoid Virginia, the younger Calvert chose to stop at the colony anyway. Many of the Virginia colonists welcomed the new arrivals, but others were not so friendly. These Virginians *"wanted noething more then our ruine,"* wrote White. In Virginia, Leonard hired Captain Henry Fleet to guide them to Maryland. Fleet had spent the past few years trading in the area. He had also spent five years as a captive of the Nacotchtank, during which time he learned how to speak the Algonquian language.

On March 25, Fleet led the settlers up the Potomac River to an island that Leonard named St. Clement's. On the island, the women cleaned the laundry while the men put together a barge made out of wooden pieces brought from England. Once the barge was built, a party began exploring the region.

To establish peaceful relations with the Indians of the region, Governor Calvert immediately sought out the Piscataway and the Yaocomaco. The Piscataway tayac welcomed the newcomers, telling them, *"We will use one table; my attendants shall go hunt for you, and all things shall be common with us."*

In exchange for weapons, tools, and cloth, the Yaocomaco granted the English settlers land on the eastern bank of St. Mary's River. The new arrivals named the settlement St. Marys City. The Yaocomaco people left their village, giving the colonists rough houses to live in and already-planted fields.

One reason the local native groups were so willing to accept the new arrivals was that they hoped the Europeans would help protect them from hostile Indians to the north, especially the Susquehannock. Although the colonists would provide some protection, they also introduced smallpox and other European diseases. In the coming years, the numbers of native people in the region would decline due to these diseases. The colonists also sped the decline of the local tribes by taking their fishing and hunting lands, destroying their crops, and committing outright violence against them.

smallpox—a contagious disease caused by a virus

FOUNDING ST. MARYS CITY

After moving from St. Clement's Island to St. Marys City, the Maryland colonists set to work improving their new home. The first task was to make their community safe from Indian attacks and hostile Spanish and French troops. They built a palisade around the settlement for protection and placed seven cannon, brought from England, inside. Later, when it became clear that the settlers could protect themselves, some moved to other areas and started their own plantations.

palisade—a high wall made out of upright logs woven tightly together

plantation—a large, self-sufficient farm

This image, drawn by historians and archaeologists studying the history of Maryland, illustrates what St. Marys City probably looked like in the early part of the 17th century.

Most of the colonists had been granted 100 acres from Cecilius. Those who brought servants received an additional 100 acres for each servant. Wives were also awarded 100 acres, while 50 acres were granted for each child under the age of 16. The settlers were allowed to choose their own land, and the best pieces (usually those along the waterways that served as Maryland's roads) went first.

In return for the land, Lord Baltimore was to be paid a yearly fee, called a quitrent. The payment could be made in wheat, corn, or tobacco. Although the quitrent would cause problems in the future,

quitrent—a tax on land

right now the generous offer of land and the promise of religious freedom attracted settlers to the new colony.

The settlers soon turned to clearing their land and building homes out of wood. And as Lord Baltimore had recommended, they quickly planted their first crops. The Maryland colonists wanted to avoid a "starving time" like the one suffered by early Virginia settlers. The Yaocomaco taught the settlers how to clear land by girdling trees. This was the practice of removing a strip of bark from around the tree so that the sap could not rise. The tree eventually died, making it easier to remove. The settlers' hard work paid off, and within the first year, they were able to export a few shipments of grain and corn from the colony to England.

On the recommendation of Virginia officials, Maryland colonists also planted a West Indian variety of tobacco that was known for its superior flavor. The colony's soil and climate were good for this crop, and the demand for tobacco in England guaranteed a market for it. Tobacco would quickly become the most important cash crop in the colony.

REINING IN A REBEL

Although Maryland's settlers had come prepared to stay and succeed, they faced a number of problems right from the start. One such problem was William Claiborne, who had left England to settle in Virginia in 1621.

In August 1631, Claiborne established the first English settlement in Maryland. He chose Kent Island, a large island in Chesapeake Bay, as a site for a trading post and town. At the post, Claiborne traded English goods for animal furs and hides with the Native Americans of the region. He also sold corn to English colonies in the north. The town around the trading post was home to about a hundred people, who had planted crops and orchards and cleared pastures for grazing livestock.

When Claiborne learned that Kent Island was now under Lord Baltimore's control, he was furious. When Maryland officials sent him notice that he was living in Maryland's domain, he responded with a letter saying that he refused to recognize the English lord's claim to the island.

On April 23, 1635, two armed Maryland ships confronted one of Claiborne's armed trading vessels in the southern part of the bay. Claiborne surrendered after a number of his men were killed. The event is sometimes called the first naval battle in U.S. history. Two years after the battle, a force from Maryland landed on Kent Island and arrested

An illustration of the battle in the waters of Chesapeake Bay between Lord Baltimore's armed vessels and William Claiborne's ships. Baltimore's victory ended the dispute between Claiborne and the Calverts over ownership of the region.

rebel leaders there. Claiborne finally agreed to recognize Governor Leonard Calvert's authority, but he was not happy about it. In the future, Claiborne would cause even more problems for Maryland officials.

PROBLEMS WITH THE PROPRIETOR

In addition to worrying about Claiborne, the absent Lord Baltimore (Cecilius) soon realized that controlling his distant colony would be a problem. He believed that the royal charter granted him the right to make all laws for his colony. However, many of the settlers had a different interpretation. They believed that the charter gave them the right to create laws, then submit them to the proprietor for approval.

The colonial government created by the charter was the provincial assembly. The first meeting of the assembly was held in St. Marys City in February 1635. At the

proprietor—a person given ownership and control of a colony

meeting, the colonists tried to write their own laws, based on laws in England. Although Governor Calvert immediately objected, the laws were sent to Lord Baltimore in England for approval. Finally, in April 1637, the colonists heard from their proprietor. He wrote, *"We do disassent to all their laws, by them heretofore . . . made within our said province, and do hereby declare them to be void."*

SHAPING MARYLAND'S GOVERNMENT

AT FIRST, MARYLAND'S COLONIAL assembly included any qualified freeman who attended the meeting. In 1639, Lord Baltimore altered the makeup of the assembly. He directed that the five settlement areas in the colony—Kent Island, St. Clements, St. Marys, St. Georges, and St. Michaels— would send a total of eight delegates to represent them. The governor would also appoint five men to act as the Council of State, a group that almost always represented the proprietor's best interests. By 1650, the assembly and the council had evolved into two houses, or sections, that met and voted separately.

He also sent a list of new laws that he had written, which he ordered the assembly to enact.

The colonists were eager to show that they could not be bullied. When they met again in January 1638, they voted to reject Lord Baltimore's laws. Then they wrote their own, incorporating several of the proprietor's suggestions. The assembly included a law that made William Claiborne an outlaw and ordered the confiscation of his land and goods. The proprietor eventually accepted these new laws and the right of the assembly to draw them up.

These early battles between Lord Baltimore and his Maryland colonists were just the first of many. In the coming decades, the proprietor and his heirs would battle Maryland's colonists for control of the colony. ✾

CHAPTER THREE

Life in the New Colony

DESPITE EFFORTS TO ATTRACT SETTLERS *from England and other parts of Europe, Lord Baltimore's colony grows slowly. Many of the earliest colonists come to Maryland as indentured servants.*

hile Lord Baltimore was dealing with the problems of running a colony from afar, Maryland's first colonists were working to survive and prosper. Most of Maryland's earliest citizens were poor folk, looking for the chance to make a better life for themselves.

The earliest colonists lived in much more primitive conditions than what they had left in England. The first

OPPOSITE: A hand-colored woodcut shows Native Americans in the region of St. Marys City sharing their food and game with the early settlers of Maryland.

homes in the colony were small, one-room houses. Few were larger than 16 feet by 20 feet (5 m by 6 m) in size. Colonists used fresh wood cut from the forests to build their homes. The wallboards shrank as they dried and aged, leaving gaps in the walls. In winter, the colonists patched the gaps with clay to keep the wind out. Roofs were shingled with wooden tiles, and a clay chimney was usually attached to the end of the house.

Inside these small homes, most colonists had a dirt floor. Settlers with a little money might buy a rug to throw over the dirt or lay wooden planking in the room. Early settlers owned few pieces of furniture, and what little furniture they had could be easily stored away during the day to clear more room in the house. For example, some settlers used heaps of

What's in the House?

EARLY MARYLAND COLONISTS brought only a few absolute necessities with them from England. Even as the colony grew, few poor or middle-class people could afford furniture. In St. Mary's in the middle and late 1600s, for example, only about one out of three households had a table, and more than half of middle-class Marylanders had no chairs. Wealthier planters, of course, owned more items, but these were not necessarily of fine quality. But even these people most often chose to invest money in their farms rather than buy unnecessary household goods.

straw or rags as beds that could be thrown in a corner during the day. Others slept on mattresses that could be rolled up and stored in the home's loft. A large chest served as a seat and a table as well as a storage place. When settlers needed more space, they usually added outbuildings, such as summer kitchens and storage sheds.

Maryland settlers plant corn on land they cleared in a pine forest along the coast of Maryland.

In 1656, John Hammond wrote a pamphlet intended to attract settlers to Maryland. He described the huts as "*contrived so delightfull, that your ordinary houses in England are not so handsome, for usually the rooms are large . . . and if not glazed [glass] windows, shutters which are made very pritty and convenient.*" However, not everyone agreed with Hammond. One visitor to the region wrote, "*The dwellings are so wretchedly constructed that if you are not so close to the fire as almost to burn yourself, you cannot keep warm, for the wind blows through them everywhere.*"

Colonial women were usually in charge of domestic chores. This drawing shows a settler washing laundry outside a building that is probably a tavern.

During the colony's earliest years, men outnumbered women by four to one. As a result, women were in high demand, and some historians believe that they may have enjoyed a "*more favorable position in family life*" than in other colonies. Wives sometimes worked alongside their husbands sharing the difficult jobs of planting tobacco and tending livestock. They also tended kitchen vegetable gardens and took care of domestic chores such as cooking, cleaning, and caring for the children.

ADJUSTING TO A
NEW CLIMATE

Maryland's earliest settlers knew that they would have to work hard to be successful in the new colony. But few realized that they would have to go through a "seasoning" that might cost them their lives. Seasoning is the body's process of adjusting to a new climate and environment.

English settlers in Maryland had to adjust to hot, humid summers, where temperatures could climb to more than 90°F (32°C). And although Maryland's winter temperatures were usually mild, sometimes they dropped below freezing, and blizzards were not uncommon. John Smith described the Maryland winter: *"The cold is extream sharp."*

epidemic—the rapid spread of disease to a large population of people

malaria—a disease spread by the bite of certain mosquitoes

diphtheria—a disease caused by bacteria that affects the throat

yellow fever—an infectious disease caused by the bite of certain mosquitoes

A new diet based on corn as well as epidemics of disease threatened the survival of many. In the bay's marshes and along the rivers, mosquitoes spread malaria. Other feared diseases included smallpox, diphtheria, yellow fever, and influenza (flu). Maryland suffered its first flu epidemic in 1675, with another serious epidemic ten years later.

The mortality rate in Maryland was much higher than in some of the other Colonies. Most young men who made the journey to the colony in their late teens

ONE MAN'S SEASONING

EBENEZER COOKE WAS BORN IN London and emigrated to Maryland as a young man. In a poem he titled "The Sotweed Factor, or A Voyage to Maryland, a Satyr," Cooke complained of the many ills that new colonists might suffer in Maryland, including seasoning:

A fiery Pulse beat in my Veins
From Cold I felt resembling
This curses seasoning [season]
I remember,
Lasted from March to cold
December. . . .
But thanks to fortune and a Nurse
Whose Care depended on my Purse,
I saw myself in good Condition,
Without the help of a Physitian.

died within 25 years. Half of all children born in Maryland during the 1600s died before the age of 20. And in one county, half of all marriages lasted just seven years before one partner died.

INDENTURED SERVANTS

Between 1640 and 1680, most of the people who settled in Maryland were indentured servants. Indentured servants signed a contract agreeing to work for a master for a certain number of years (usually four to six) in return for passage to the American colonies, along with "Meat, Drinke, Apparel and Lodging, with other necessaries." Some signed their contract before they set sail.

Most of the indentured servants who came to Maryland were young, single men who were illiterate. All of them were poor. In London and other English cities, agents called "spirits" frequented taverns and poor neighborhoods, looking for young men willing to emigrate to America. Other immigrants shipped across the Atlantic Ocean with the hope of being hired when they got to Maryland. The captain who brought the servants was paid by the masters who "bought" them.

Once they had been sold into service, indentured servants truly became the property of their masters. Following English custom,

> The forme of binding a fervant.
>
> **T**his **Indenture** *made the*   *day of*
>   *in the*
> *yeere of our Soveraigne Lord King* Charles, &c.
> *betweene*   *of the one*
> *party, and*   *on the*
> *other party,* Witneffeth, *that the faid*
>   *doth hereby covenant promife, and*
> *grant, to and with the faid*
> *his Executors and Affignes, to ferve him from the*
> *day of the date hereof, vntill his firft and next arri-*
> *vall in* Maryland; *and after for and during the*
> *tearme of*   *yeeres, in fuch fervice and imploy-*
> *ment, as the faid*   *or his*
> *affignes fhall there imploy him, according to the cuf-*
> *tome of the Countrey in the like kind. In confidera-*
> *tion whereof, the faid*
> *doth promife and grant, to and with the faid*
>   *to pay for his paffing,*
> *and to find him with Meat, Drinke, Apparell and*
> *Lodging, with other neceffaries during the faid terme;*
> *and at the end of the faid terme, to give him one*
> *whole yeeres provifion of Corne, and fifty acres of*
>   *Land,*

A copy of a blank contract between an indentured servant and his employer lays out the terms of payment for the servant's passage to Maryland and the items he will be granted (corn and 50 acres of land) upon completion of his service.

they were required to work as many as 14 hours each day (although they did not work Saturday afternoons and Sundays). The master controlled their personal life, too. As long as their contract lasted, servants could not marry.

Men and women indentured to a cruel master might spend the next years of their lives in misery. Masters were allowed, by law, to beat lazy or defiant servants in order to

Views on
a Servant's Life

IN AN EFFORT TO ENCOURAGE MORE INDENTURED SERVANTS to come to Maryland, colonist John Hammond wrote a description of the easy life awaiting them:

The labour servants are put to, is not so hard . . . as I said little or nothing is done in winter time, none ever work before sun rising nor after sun set, in the summer they rest, sleep or exercise themselves five houres in the heat of the day, Saturdayes afternoon is always their own, the old Holidayes are observed and the Sabboath spent in good exercises.

Yet in 1679 two travelers recorded very different observations about the life of indentured servants in the colony:

[They have] maize bread to eat, and water to drink, which sometimes is not very good and scarcely enough for life, yet they are compelled to work hard. . . .The servants . . . after they have worn themselves down the whole day, and gone home to rest, have yet to grind and pound the grain, which is generally maize, for their masters and all their families as well as themselves.

"correct" them. Runaways were severely punished. Another way that masters punished their servants for real or alleged wrongdoing was to extend their term of service. Some unscrupulous planters extended a servant's indenture for several years. Servants who took a cruel master to court usually found little protection for themselves under the law.

Once their terms of service had ended, servants were usually given land, clothes, and a year's supply of corn. Some former indentured servants found success in Maryland. One such person was Zachary Wade, a former servant of Margaret Brent. Wade was able to buy 4,000 acres (1,620 ha) of land over a period of about 30 years after completing his indenture. When he died in 1678, he was one of the largest landowners and one of the wealthiest men in the colony. Other former indentured servants in Maryland held public office and bought smaller chunks of land.

However, most indentured servants were not as lucky as Wade. Those who arrived early in the colony's history generally fared well if they stayed healthy. Before 1642, more than half ended up owning their own land. After 1670, however, with the best land taken, the chances for success dwindled. Only a handful of indentured servants went on to become wealthy. Many simply disappeared from colonial records. These people may have died, moved to another colony, or returned to England. Others may have remained in Maryland as tenant farmers.

tenant farmer—a person who rents land in order to farm it

This map shows the eastern portion of Maryland Colony in 1670. According to its 1632 charter,
it included all of present-day Delaware and a strip of southern Pennsylvania (see inset map),
neither of which existed as English colonies at the time. Until John Smith's exploratory voyages
of Chesapeake Bay in 1608 and 1609 opened the region to European settlement, the land belonged
to the Piscataways, Choptanks, and other Algonquian peoples labeled on the map, as it had for
thousands of years. Choice land on the eastern and western shores of the bay was snapped up by
colonists and turned into large English farms. The colony's first counties all bordered the bay.
Providence, a Puritan settlement near the northern end of Chesapeake Bay, would be renamed
Annapolis and replace St. Marys as Maryland's capital in 1694.

By 1642, Maryland had grown to about 400 people, most of them located around St. Marys City. This settlement area became known as St. Marys County. The county itself was divided into smaller sections, known as hundreds. Each hundred had a constable who kept order in the district.

Many of the largest landowners were the original Catholic lords who had settled there in 1634. In 1642, the largest "manorial lord," or large plantation owner, was Catholic council member Thomas Gerard. Gerard owned more than 6,000 acres (2,430 ha) of land, including St. Clements Island where the first colonists aboard the *Ark* and the *Dove* landed.

freemen—people, excluding indentured servants, Native Americans, slaves, and women, having the full rights of citizenship

Other planters in Maryland owned much smaller plantations. Many landless freemen also lived in the colony. Although Lord Baltimore still offered land grants, many poor colonists did not have the money for tools, seeds, and other supplies needed to farm their own land. As a result, many chose to rent plots of land from the large landowners. ❋

CHAPTER FOUR

The Time of Troubles

MARYLAND'S CATHOLIC-LED GOVERNMENT *is briefly over-thrown. To satisfy Protestants in the colony, Lord Baltimore appoints a Protestant governor, and the colonial assembly passes an act to protect religious freedom.*

In 1642, events across the Atlantic caused serious problems in Maryland. That year, the English Civil War began. The war pitted supporters of King Charles, called Royalists, against supporters of England's Parliament, sometimes called Roundheads. (Many men who supported Parliament were Puritans who sported short haircuts instead of the fashionable long hair

OPPOSITE: The leader of the Puritan forces (carrying the flag) charges at Governor Stone (center with feathered hat) and his forces at the mouth of the Severn River. Stone was fighting to preserve Catholic leadership and religious tolerance in the Maryland colony, but in less than half an hour his forces were defeated.

worn by aristocrats, hence the name round-heads.) Puritans were zealous Protestants who were even more anti-Catholic than other Protestant English people. After four years of conflict, the Roundhead forces defeated the Royalists. In January 1647, Charles became a prisoner of Parliament.

Parliament—England's lawmaking body

Puritan—a Protestant in the 1500s and 1600s who advocated strict morals and simple worship services

One strong supporter of Parliament during the war was Puritan Richard Ingle. Ingle, a ship captain, had become wealthy by carrying trade goods between England and Maryland. During the war, Ingle arrived in Maryland with papers from Parliament that authorized him to seize Royalist ships. Giles Brent, serving as temporary governor while Calvert visited Virginia, ignored these papers. When Ingle remarked, *"The King is no King,"* Brent had the English captain arrested for treason. Ingle's sympathizers succeeded in getting him released from prison. He returned to his ship and fled to England.

Ingle was back in February 1645, this time with a well-armed ship. Ingles and his band marched into St. Marys City and took control of the colonial government. Governor Calvert had wisely fled to safety in Virginia. Ingle destroyed government records and Lord Baltimore's seal, which was used by the governor to make documents and decrees official.

Next, Ingle demanded that all Maryland citizens take an *"oath of submission"* to Parliament. Those who refused—

whether Catholic or Protestant—had their homes and farms destroyed. Ingle's men killed livestock, burned fences, and even took door locks and window glass from homes.

During Ingle's Rebellion, William Claiborne, who had been outlawed by the colonial assembly for his opposition to the proprietor, took advantage of the chaos to seize control of the trading post on Kent Island. His return was short-lived, however. In December 1646, Governor Calvert was finally able to raise a force of soldiers by promising to pay them (using his own money) after order was restored in Maryland. But by the time they arrived in St. Marys City, Ingle had headed back to England, and Claiborne had returned to Virginia.

Governor Calvert now began the task of returning peace to the colony. In June 1647, however, he suddenly sickened and died. Leonard Calvert, just 41 years old, had spent the last 13 years of his life protecting his brother's interests in Maryland. Before his death, Calvert named Margaret Brent, a landowner whose family was a political ally of Lord Baltimore, as his executor.

executor—someone who is selected to make sure a person's will and last wishes are followed

Margaret Brent soon learned that Calvert had promised to pay his soldiers from his own funds. The men were demanding payment and threatening to riot if they did not get their money. To prevent yet another rebellion within the colony, Brent sold the governor's belongings and land. When the money raised still did not cover Calvert's debt, she sold some of her own property as well as some belonging to Lord Baltimore.

Although Brent's quick thinking and cool head had saved the colony from another outbreak of violence, Lord Baltimore was not pleased. The proprietor sent a letter to the assembly that criticized her actions. The assembly, which supported Brent, wrote back,

> As for Mistress Brent's undertaking and medling with your Lordships Estate . . . we do Verily Believe and in Conscience report, that it was better for the collonys safety at that time in her hands than in any mans else in the whole Province. . . . she rather deserved favour and thanks from your Honour for her so much Concurring to the publick safety then to be justly liable to all those bitter invectives [abusive language] you have been pleased to Express against her.

A PROTESTANT GOVERNOR

While Margaret Brent was worrying about how to pay Calvert's soldiers, civil war was once again dividing England. In 1647, Charles I escaped his captors and mounted an attack against Parliament. By the summer of 1648, the king had been defeated for the final time.

After the Royalists' defeat, Lord Baltimore tried to appease the Puritans, now led by Oliver Cromwell by appointing Virginian William Stone as the first Protestant governor of Maryland. One of Stone's first actions was to invite a group of 300 Puritans who were being persecuted in Virginia to move to Maryland. The leader of the group, Richard Bennett, had been banished from Virginia for preaching in the colony. He and his Puritan followers founded a settlement called Providence at the mouth of the Severn River on Maryland's Western Shore.

WOMAN SUFFRAGE
in the 1600s

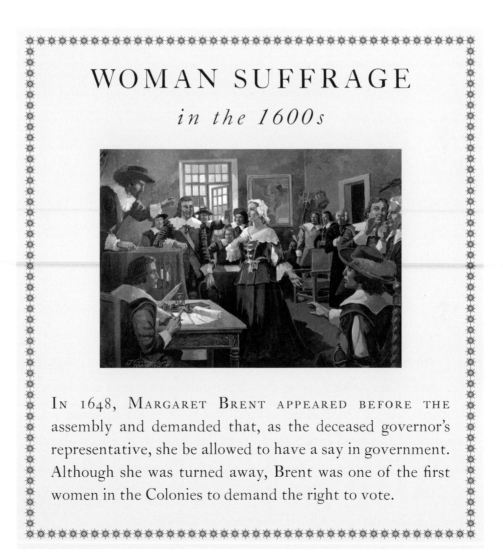

IN 1648, MARGARET BRENT APPEARED BEFORE THE assembly and demanded that, as the deceased governor's representative, she be allowed to have a say in government. Although she was turned away, Brent was one of the first women in the Colonies to demand the right to vote.

Maryland became even more attractive to persecuted religious groups after April 1649, when the colonial assembly passed a law ordering there to be freedom of religion. The law was called "An Act Concerning Religion," but it became better known as the Toleration Act. It guaranteed colonists the right to worship as they pleased and fined those who spoke out against the religion of others. The new law promised that no Christian would *"bee any wais troubled [or] molested . . . for or in respect of his or her religion nor in the free exercise thereof . . . nor any way compelled to the beleife or exercise of any other Religion against his or her consent."*

The Toleration Act was the first law passed by an English-speaking colony to ensure toleration for all Christians, but it did not mention or include those of other religious faiths. In the coming years, people from various religious groups would come to Maryland hoping to enjoy religious freedom. The Toleration Act would help pave the way for freedoms that would be set forth for all the Colonies in the future Declaration of Independence.

Soon after the passage of the Toleration Act, word reached the colony that Cromwell's forces had captured King Charles. In January 1649, he was tried for treason, found guilty, and beheaded. For the next 9 years, Oliver Cromwell controlled England as Lord Protector. Although a staunch Puritan, Cromwell was willing to work with Lord Baltimore to keep the peace in Maryland.

Oliver Cromwell, the Puritan leader who controlled
England's Parliament from 1653 to 1658

THE PURITANS GAIN STRENGTH

In late 1649, Governor Stone left Maryland just long
enough for his deputy governor, Thomas Greene, to stir up
trouble with the Puritans. Instead of recognizing
Cromwell's authority, Greene followed Virginia's lead in
proclaiming Charles II, son of the executed king, the
sovereign of England. When Parliament learned of the
action of the two Chesapeake colonies, it appointed
Puritan leader Richard Bennett and old foe William
Claiborne to take charge of the two colonies.

When the men arrived in St. Marys in 1652, they decided to leave the Protestant governor in office for the time being. But in July 1654, Bennett and Claiborne removed Stone from office. To govern the colony, they created a ten-member council made up of Puritans. This new council, it was decided, would meet at Patuxent, away from the Catholic stronghold of St. Marys City.

Soon after the Puritan council took over, it repealed the Toleration Act. In October 1654, a new law banned Roman Catholics from openly practicing their religion. The council also did away with the oath of loyalty that landowners were required to swear to the proprietor. Other laws passed by the council included bans on swearing, drunkenness, slander, adultery, and other vices.

slander—the act of speaking falsely about a person in order to harm him or her

adultery—the act of being unfaithful to one's wife or husband

Lord Baltimore asked Oliver Cromwell for help in taking control of his rebellious colony. Cromwell agreed, sending a message to the Puritans to *"forbear disturbing the Lord Baltimore or his officers or people in Maryland, and to permit all things to remain as they were before any disturbance or alteration made by you, or by any other upon pretence of authority from you."*

In March 1655, Governor Stone led 100 men in an attack on the Puritan stronghold of Providence. However, the Puritans had a larger force, and they easily defeated Stone and his troops. During the Battle of the Severn, the governor lost about half his men. After his troops surrendered, the Puritans executed a small number of prisoners, and Stone and his council were imprisoned for more than a month.

In November 1657, Lord Baltimore, Richard Bennett, and William Claiborne signed a peace agreement. According to the agreement, Bennett and Claiborne recognized the proprietor's right to rule the colony and agreed to support religious toleration. For his part, the English lord agreed not to punish the two men for their part in the Puritan rebellion. For the next 30 years, the Calvert family would remain in charge of Maryland.

The Restoration

IN 1658, OLIVER CROMWELL died and his government began to fall apart. Two years later, England's monarchy was restored, and Charles II, son of the executed king, took the throne. The period of Charles II's reign became known as the Restoration.

CHAPTER FIVE

Tobacco and Struggle

MARYLAND'S ECONOMY GROWS SLOWLY, *boosted by the success of tobacco plantations. New arrivals make their homes on both the Western and Eastern Shores, but unrest continues to plague the colony.*

hroughout the years of chaos and rebellion in Maryland, settlers continued to come to the colony. People from England fled to Maryland and other Colonies to escape the civil war, high prices, and a lack of economic opportunities. By 1660, the colony's population had climbed to about 2,500.

OPPOSITE: A colonist smoking a variety of tobacco called Old Maryland. Tobacco, the colony's most important crop, created a wealthy class of planters who owned slaves and employed indentured servants to work the fields.

LIFE ON THE CHESAPEAKE

From the earliest years of Maryland's history, tobacco was the most important crop in the colony. Most of the free male colonists were tobacco planters, growing and selling the crop for a good profit. Only a handful of the planters owned large plantations, however. Most of them were small farmers who sold their tobacco to larger planters who had resources to export their tobacco.

Tobacco cultivation required much care and hard work. The process began in the late winter or early spring, when planters seeded their fields. To protect the newly sown seeds from frost, they were covered with cloth. Once warmer weather arrived, the seedlings were transplanted into mounds of soil. Then the plants were carefully tended. The planter and his help had to work the fields constantly, making sure to remove grubs and other pests that could ruin the crop.

In late summer, the leaves of the ripe plant were cut, tied to sticks, and hung to dry in big, airy tobacco barns. The drying had to be carefully managed. If the tobacco was still damp when packed, it would rot in the hogshead. The entire process took most of the year, from February to November.

hogshead—a large barrel used to transport tobacco or other goods

Most of the planters hired indentured servants to help with the backbreaking labor of tending the crops. On small plantations, the master and his family worked and lived side by side with the indentured servants. Although African slaves were used on larger plantations, they were still out-numbered by white servants.

The plantations benefited from the many waterways that emptied into the big bay. Hogsheads of tobacco were transported from small plantations to large ones by small boats. Planters who lived a distance from a waterway would roll the hogsheads down a rough path to the nearest dock. As a result, these early colonial roads became known as rolling roads.

Bringing tobacco to market was a difficult process because the plants had to be kept dry. The rolling roads had to be kept free of rocks and roots in order to make a smooth path for the large, sturdy barrels known as hogsheads.

The largest planters were the colony's elite. Many became merchants, importing goods from Europe and selling them to smaller planters. By extending credit for these goods and offering loans, the big planters also became the colony's first bankers. Many were often in debt themselves to merchants in London.

WEST AND EAST

Before 1650, most of Maryland's colonists settled on the Western Shore. Early colonists settled in the vicinity of St. Marys City, with newcomers pushing farther into Maryland's interior. By 1660, four new counties had been created on the Western Shore: Anne Arundel, Baltimore, Calvert, and Charles. Within the next ten years, the western arm of the bay had a population of about 13,000 people.

Although St. Marys City was the oldest settlement in Maryland—and the colonial capital—it had not grown into an important urban area. By 1678, St. Marys City had just 30 houses, which stood as far as 6 miles (10 km) away from each other. Easy access to the Chesapeake and other waterways allowed waterfront towns to have their own docks and markets. As a result, no central, thriving trade center developed in the colony. Most of Maryland's settlements were hamlets (small villages) not towns or cities.

Only one county, Kent, had been created on the colony's Eastern Shore. After 1650, however, increasing numbers of settlers chose to make their homes on the eastern side of the bay. By 1668, Governor Charles Calvert, Lord Baltimore's son, who had taken office in 1661, had established three new counties there: Talbot, Somerset, and Dorchester.

By 1680, emigration to Maryland had tapered off due to a long economic depression that gripped the colony. The demand for Maryland tobacco had dwindled. Large planters struggled to survive, and many small planters failed. Some colonists left Maryland at this time, migrating to Pennsylvania, the Carolinas, Delaware, and New Jersey. Many of those who left were former indentured servants, unable to make a good living in Maryland.

TROUBLE WITH THE TRIBES

With Lord Baltimore officially again in charge of Maryland, his representatives began working to bring peace to the colony. One of their first tasks was to deal with the Native Americans in the region. In the years since St. Marys City was founded, relations between some tribes and the settlers had deteriorated. The early alliances that Lord Baltimore worked so hard to achieve crumbled as settlers took over more and more land and competed with the natives for fish, game, and land for planting. Settlers struck back by attacking Indians and further destroying their crops. Alcohol, which the settlers traded to the tribes in exchange for skins also caused violence and other problems in Indian groups.

Tribes from outside the region also created problems in the colony. The Seneca and the Iroquois waged war on Maryland Indians, attacking colonial settlements in the process. Devastated by smallpox and other European diseases, the Piscataway and other local tribes could not defend themselves against the larger native groups.

In 1660, Marylanders declared war on the Iroquois, one of the hostile tribes from the north. To raise money to build fortresses and pay the colonial militia, Governor Charles Calvert imposed a tax on each hogshead of tobacco, which made the already dwindling market even worse. The colonists were furious. They thought that Lord Baltimore should use the money he earned from quitrents to fund the war.

militia—a group of citizen-soldiers

Native Americans and Maryland colonists battle over trade issues in this illustration of one of many skirmishes that made up the Nanticoke War.

In 1675, Maryland again found itself at war with the Indians, this time with the Nanticoke. The war had actually started in Virginia when misunderstandings over trade led to theft and murder. In order to punish the Nanticoke, Virginia's militia crossed into Maryland and attacked a native village. About 25 Nanticoke and Susquehannock people were killed. In retaliation, the Indians began raiding both Virginia and Maryland settlements, causing destruction and killing colonists. Eventually a peace treaty ended the conflict, sometimes known as the Nanticoke War.

RETURN TO REBELLION

Conflicts with the Native Americans were not the only problem in Maryland during the 1660s and 1670s. The entire colonial economy was suffering from a drop in tobacco prices. When the assembly tried to pass a law to limit tobacco production for a year in order to boost prices, Lord Baltimore vetoed the law, saying that it would *"wholly ruine the poor who are the [majority]...."* The veto, along with the recent changes in the way land was granted and the new taxes, made the assembly and the colonists unhappy with the proprietor and his government.

In 1675, Cecilius Calvert, the second Lord Baltimore, died in England. Not once in 40 years had he visited Maryland. Now his son, Governor Charles Calvert, would become the third Lord Baltimore and inherit complete control of the colony.

Soon after his father's death, Charles Calvert headed back to England to put the family's affairs in order. Unhappy colonists in Calvert County took the opportunity of the governor's absence to complain publicly about proprietary rule. In a pamphlet called "Complaint from Heaven

Charles Calvert, the third Lord Baltimore, was made governor of Maryland in 1675.

with a Huy and Crye . . . out of Virginia and Maryland," the colonists listed their grievances against the Calverts and the colony's Catholic officials. The long, rambling letter, addressed to King Charles II, claimed that the poor colonists were being "robbed" and "cheated" by their superiors. The writers also accused the Calverts of conspiring with the French and the Indians during the recent Nanticoke War. They begged the king to take control of Maryland and make it a Protestant colony.

The same year, an Anglican minister named John Yeo penned his own assessment of life in colonial Maryland. Yeo wrote, *"The province of Maryland is in a deplorable condition. . . . The Lord's day is profaned. Religion is despised, and all notorious vices are committed; so that it is become a Sodom of uncleanliness and a pest house of iniquity."* Virginia's governor also described the situation in the colony as disastrous: *"Maryland is now in torment, and not only troubled with our disease, poverty, but in very great danger of falling in pieces."*

Anglican—a member of the Protestant Church of England; also the official religion of the English government

The written complaints were a warning of stronger action to come. In 1688, the simmering tensions between Protestant colonists, represented by the assembly, and the Catholic proprietors, represented by the council, boiled over. That year, William Joseph, a Catholic, was appointed governor of the colony by Lord Baltimore. When Joseph addressed the assembly in November, he insisted that the proprietor had the absolute right to rule in Maryland. The following year, the governor refused to open the assembly and ordered all counties to return their weapons to St. Marys "for repair."

The same month that Governor Joseph was antagonizing the assembly, the Catholic King James II (the son of Charles I and brother of Charles II) was overthrown in the Glorious Rebellion. His Protestant daughter, Mary, and her husband, the Dutch Protestant William of Orange, were invited to invade England and take control of the throne, which they did in December 1688. Under the reign of William and Mary, laws were passed to prevent a Roman Catholic from ever again sitting on the throne of England.

In July 1689, a group known as the Protestant Association rose up in Charles County, Maryland, and rebelled. The group's leader was John Coode, a former member of the assembly and a violent opponent of proprietary rule. The Associators, as Coode and his followers became known, issued a "Declaration of the reasons and motive for

Associators—an anti-Catholic, anti-proprietor group led by John Coode the present appearing in arms of His Majesties Protestant Subjects in the Province of Maryland." Like past documents, the pamphlet listed grievances against the Catholic proprietor and again asked that the English monarch take control of the colony.

PROFILE

John Coode

According to a number of people who knew him, John Coode was an unpleasant, controversial character. Coode had emigrated to the Colonies from England when he was a young man. He served as an Anglican minister until he was expelled from his position. In the early 1670s, he was jailed for debt. In later years, however, he married a wealthy widow and was elected to the assembly. He was removed from the assembly after plotting to overthrow the proprietor.

In 1689, Coode served a brief term as Maryland's governor. However, the end of his life was marked by more turmoil. He took part in two more rebellions against the government and was eventually put on trial for blasphemy. The court sentenced him to have his tongue bored through with a hot poker, but Coode was pardoned by Governor Blackston, who believed his service to Maryland entitled him to go free. He died in 1709.

In July, the Associators armed themselves and began marching toward St. Marys City, determined to take control of the government, by force if necessary. As they approached the capital, more angry colonists joined them. When the group of 700 men arrived at St. Marys, the council quickly surrendered without a shot being fired. Proprietary rule had once more been overthrown in Maryland. ❈

CHAPTER SIX

A Growing Colony

Laws to protect religious freedom in the royal colony are repealed and the capital is moved to Annapolis. The use of slave labor skyrockets as the tobacco industry flourishes. By 1715, the Calverts are once again given control of Maryland.

oode's Rebellion in 1689 resulted in Maryland becoming a royal colony. King William took over ownership and governance of the colony. In 1692, the first royal governor, Lionel Copley, arrived in Maryland. The colony would remain under direct royal control for nearly 25 years.

OPPOSITE: Slaves on a large plantation were often given a piece of pasture to farm for themselves. This illustration shows Africans working land in front of housing provided for them by their master. Slaves grew crops to feed their families or grazed cattle they had been given for milk. A few slave owners allowed slaves to sell whatever they cultivated on their plots.

RELIGIOUS INTOLERANCE

New laws were quickly passed to reflect the change in leadership. Anglicanism became the colony's official religion, as it was in England, and religious tolerance quickly ended. In 1692, the assembly passed the Act for the Service of Almighty God and the Establishment of the Protestant Religion within this Province. The new law, aimed at *"wicked Lewd and disorderly people,"* outlawed *"drunkenness, Swearing, Gaming, fowling [bird hunting], fishing hunting, or any other Sports Pastimes or Recreations whatsoever"* on Sundays. Violations could result in penalties ranging from fines to branding to whipping to death. All non-Anglicans were now required to pay a tax to support Anglican churches in the colony. Those who refused to pay the tax could be jailed or fined.

Quakers, Presbyterians, Puritans, and Catholics who refused to take an oath of loyalty to the king and his religion were no longer permitted to hold office. As a result, many Quakers and Catholics were excluded from the assembly and from juries. Later, Catholics who refused to take the oath were denied the right to vote. Quakers were further targeted with laws that banned the court testimony of any person who refused to swear an oath of allegiance to the proprietor. Colonial laws also punished Quakers (who didn't believe in warfare) by refusing to exempt them from serving in the colonial militia.

Quaker—a member of the Protestant religious group called the Society of Friends

Presbyterian—a member of a Protestant group formed in the 1500s in Switzerland

A New Governor, A New Capital

When Governor Copley died in 1693, he was replaced by Francis Nicholson, an Anglican who had served as lieutenant governor in both New England and Virginia. Nicholson's firm leadership would provide stability and allow the colony to grow steadily in the coming years.

One of the new governor's first acts was to move the colonial capital to a site near a village at the mouth of the Severn River, first settled as Providence in 1649. The new capital was renamed Anne's Polis (Greek for "city"), later known as Annapolis. The new capital represented a fresh start for the colony.

Governor Nicholson took part in carefully planning the new town's growth. The town's two main hills would serve as its two circular centers. On the larger hill, colonists began constructing the statehouse and the court-house. The smaller hill was the site of the town's church. Roads radiated out from both circles, with square plots of land located around the centers.

Annapolis grew very slowly. Other than the colonial assembly, there was little to attract colonists to the town. For many years, it had only dirt roads. In 1699, a visitor said of the town, *"There are in itt about fourty dwelling houses . . . seven or eight whereof cann afford good lodging and accommodations for strangers. There is alsoe a State house and a free schoole built with bricke . . . and the foundations of a church laid, the only bricke church in Maryland. They have two market dais in the week."*

A 1718 map of Annapolis shows the two high points in town as circles with roads and plots branching out toward the borders of the city.

That same year, the Annapolis statehouse was struck by lightning, which caused serious damage to the roof and walls. Five years later, a fire destroyed the building. Many Catholics saw the fire as a sign of God's displeasure at the new government.

The move to Annapolis spelled the end of St. Marys City as a thriving colonial village. Archaeologists working at St. Marys City have recently found reminders of its former glory, however. They have uncovered trade goods that were imported during colonial times from the Netherlands, France, Italy, China, and many other countries.

THE GROWTH OF SLAVERY

By the early 1700s, about half of the landowners on Maryland's Eastern Shore were related by blood or marriage. These planters and their families came to dominate the political, economic, and social scene. They bought more land in the colony and expanded their plantations. Poorer folks in Maryland found it harder to be successful.

The number of indentured servants willing to come to Maryland had begun to drop off in the 1670s. As economic conditions improved in England, fewer poor people were willing to take their chances as indentured servants in a strange land. More and more, planters turned to African slaves for labor. Although slaves had lived in the colony since its founding, their numbers had remained small. Not until 1695 had the first mass shipment of slaves been brought into the colony. Between 1670 and 1700, however, the number of slaves in the colony grew from 2,000 to 13,000.

By 1720, the number of enslaved people brought into Maryland began to decline. Instead, the population of slaves grew through births. By 1776, in some counties of Maryland, about one person out of every four was black. Most of the black population was enslaved. The few free blacks were usually the children of white men and enslaved women.

Evidence of slavery in Maryland can be found in some of the colony's earliest laws. In 1664, for example, the assembly passed a law stating that black people were slaves for life and that their condition was hereditary. This meant that the children of enslaved people would also be slaves. In the late 1600s and early 1700s, laws restricted the freedoms slaves had. In 1695, a law banned the *"frequent Assembly"* of blacks. Nine years later, the colony enacted laws that strengthened punishments for helping fugitive (runaway) slaves.

Slaves prepare tobacco for market, bundling and hanging the leaves to dry in a covered shed on a plantation.

LIFE UNDER SLAVERY

Most of the early slaves in Maryland were males. These strong, young men were brought into the colony to work on tobacco plantations. They also tended livestock, built fences, and cut trees for fuel and for building houses. Some slaves were trained as blacksmiths, carpenters, and coopers. Others, especially the few female slaves, were house slaves, per-

coopers—barrelmakers

forming domestic tasks like cleaning, cooking, and laundry.

Blacks worked side by side with white indentured servants. Although the master might have viewed both the indentured servant and the slave as his personal property, the white servant had the promise of someday being free. Enslaved people had no such future to look forward to. They were slaves for life, as were their children and grandchildren. Most colonists viewed the slaves as little better than animals.

As human property, slaves could be bought and sold. They could also be severely punished for mistakes or misdeeds. Especially difficult slaves might even be beaten to death. New slaves, according to one colonist, were the most likely to rebel against their enslavement: "*A new Negro, if he must be broke, either from Obstinacy or, which I am more apt to suppose, from [pride], will require more hard Discipline than a young Spaniel. . . . they often die before they can be conquer'd.*"

Despite this "*hard Discipline,*" some slaves found ways to rebel against their masters. Some worked slowly or found ways to destroy crops or damage tools. Others tried to escape, although the penalties for running away were severe and cruel. In the late 1720s, a group of slaves succeeded in escaping from their masters and went to live with Indians in the woods.

Other acts of rebellion were more violent. In 1739, Jack Ransom and other slaves in Prince George's County plotted to kill their masters and their families. Ransom was caught and hanged before the plan could be carried out.

Convicts chained together outside of Newgate Prison in London prepare to be transported to Maryland, where they will work as servants as punishment for their crimes.

CRIMINALS AS COLONISTS

In 1717, Great Britain began punishing its criminals by shipping them to Virginia and Maryland to work as servants. This punishment was called transportation. The convicts were transported to the Chesapeake by private merchants who sold them to the highest bidder. Some convicts viewed transportation as a fate worse than death. Saying that *"Living in foreign Parts was worse than a disgraceful and shameful Death at Home,"* thief Mary Stanford asked to be hanged.

transportation—the act of sending convicts to another country to serve their sentences by working for colonists there

During a 50-year period, 10,000 criminals were transported from Britain to Maryland. By 1755, one out of every ten males in four Maryland counties was a transportee.

A Return to Calvert Rule

As long as the Calverts remained Catholic, they had little chance of convincing the British monarchy to return control of Maryland to them. In 1713, however, Benedict Leonard Calvert, the third Lord Baltimore's son and heir, converted to Protestantism. When his father died two years later, King George I returned full proprietary rights to Benedict, now the fourth Lord Baltimore.

Just two months later, 35-year-old Benedict died. His 15-year-old son, Charles, became the fifth Lord Baltimore and the ruler of the Maryland colony. Before long, he demanded quitrents and other payments that he thought were owed to him.

Times had changed since his grandfather, the third Lord Baltimore, had controlled Maryland. The assembly, now made up of each county's wealthiest, most powerful citizens, was used to ruling the colony itself with little interference. The representatives were not willing to give up the power they had gained to the new proprietor, no matter what his religion.

The Calvert takeover marked the beginning of renewed political conflict in the colony. On Lord Baltimore's and the governor's side was the "court party," a group of supporters centered in St. Marys City. Those who opposed proprietary authority became known as the "country party." ✺

CHAPTER SEVEN

Maryland's Golden Age

MARYLAND EXPERIENCES A PERIOD *of prosperity and growth. Many of the colony's new settlers make their homes in the Piedmont, Maryland's western frontier.*

fter 1715, Maryland planters saw a gradual revival of the tobacco trade, earning better profits than they had since the 1680s.

The 1720s also marked the beginning of new settlement in Maryland. In 1729, Baltimore was founded at the head of the Patapsco River, where the waterway widened to create a large natural harbor. The new town was intended to serve as a shipping center for the tobacco trade. The waterfalls and strong currents at the fall line would also power mills to grind grain and cut wood.

OPPOSITE: Wealthy Marylanders often had portraits made of family members. Painted about 1710, this one shows Eleanor Darnall, the young daughter of a prominent Maryland planter, with her dog.

WESTERN FRONTIER

In the 1740s, people began making their homes in Maryland's western frontier, known as the Piedmont. Most of the new arrivals were immigrants from nearby Colonies or Europe. Many were German speakers from Pennsylvania and Scotch-Irish immigrants.

Piedmont—the foothills of the Appalachian Mountains in western Maryland

Settlement in the frontier was spurred by Daniel Dulany, a former indentured servant from Ireland. Dulany studied law in Charles County before becoming a lawyer and moving to Annapolis in 1722. He was elected to the assembly and was later appointed to several government offices.

Daniel Dulany

In the 1730s, Dulany began buying up large chunks of land in the western part of the colony. As immigrants from Pennsylvania and other Colonies traveled through the region in search of land, Dulany encouraged them to stop and settle there. He offered them parcels of his land at reasonable prices, and many accepted.

To promote the area's growth, Dulany founded a market town in 1745 that he named Frederick. The town quickly became a trading center for the region, as merchants, craftsmen, and others settled there. By 1750, about 1,000 people had settled in Frederick, making it the largest town in Maryland.

THE ECONOMY DIVERSIFIES

One reason for the rapid growth of new settlements in the Piedmont was the change in the colonial economy. Since the late 1600s, New England vessels had been buying Maryland grain to trade in the West Indies and sell in the markets of the northeastern colonies. Now, a number of factors pushed small farmers to grow more wheat, barley, oats, and rye. The demand and prices for these grains increased steadily after 1720. In addition, much of the new farmland being opened up in western Maryland was better suited to growing grain than tobacco. Soon, Maryland grain was being shipped to Philadelphia. From Philadelphia, the grain was sent on to markets in other Colonies and to Britain.

Baltimore benefited greatly from the economic shift toward grain. It became a major trade center, where wheat from throughout the region was brought for shipment. The new grain market also boosted Maryland's shipping industry. The forests around the town provided the wood needed for building and outfitting all types of vessels. Baltimore became home to a vibrant shipping industry that

attracted merchants, laborers, and skilled craftsmen, such
as ropemakers and carpenters.

The trade in grain also spurred the growth and prosperity of other Maryland towns. Villages developed along
the roads to Philadelphia and Baltimore and to Georgetown
and Alexandria in Virginia as merchants and innkeepers set
up shops. More towns developed between the Piedmont and
the Atlantic coastal plain as colonists built mills to grind the
wheat and other grains.

An oil painting of Mountain Lake in the Piedmont region
along Maryland's western frontier

Since John Smith's explorations, colonists had known
that Maryland had rich iron deposits. In the mid-1700s,
the assembly began offering rewards to people who would

set up iron furnaces and process the metal for sale to Britain. The British, in turn, used the iron to create finished goods such as ax heads, knives, kettles, frying pans, and cannonballs, which they sold back to the Colonies or to other countries. By the American Revolution, iron was being produced at more than 35 furnaces and forges and had become an important part of Maryland's economy.

The first iron company was the Principio Company, located in northern Maryland. The company built the colony's first iron furnace in 1720. In 1731, Dulany and other wealthy Maryland colonists founded the Baltimore Ironworks along the Patapsco River. The company produced both pig iron and bar iron. Pig iron is the raw iron that comes out of the furnace after first being cooked to remove the oxygen from the metal. Pig iron could then be heated again and poured into molds to make bars of solid iron called bar iron.

The Baltimore Ironworks, like other iron companies, used mostly slave labor. The slaves cut trees to fuel the furnaces that melted the metal. By the 1740s, the company had bought up about 30,000 acres (12,150 ha) of land and was using 150 slaves.

Despite Maryland's new industries, tobacco remained important. Farmers continued exporting the leaves in large quantities. Tobacco was also still used as money in Maryland, given to government officials in payment of taxes and other fees.

Artist William Strickland painted Baltimore Harbor as it looked in 1752, with settlements and crops along the shoreline, ships in the bay, and fishermen casting nets in the shallow waters.

A THRIVING COLONY

As the economy prospered, so did Maryland's towns and many of its citizens. Baltimore grew quickly, especially in the 1750s and 1760s when the French and Indian War increased the demand by British troops for wheat and iron from Maryland. By 1768, the thriving port town had become the county seat and had about 350 houses. As many as 80 ships called the port home.

The standard of living in colonial Maryland improved greatly during the mid-1700s. The fine homes in Baltimore and other parts of the colony little resembled the one-room cottages of the past. People began building with brick instead of wood, and the new homes were spacious and stately.

Annapolis, Maryland's capital, also flourished during the period. By the middle of the 1700s, some of the colony's wealthiest families, including the Carrolls and the Dulanys, made their homes in Annapolis. In all, about 150 households were scattered about the town. Annapolis was home to some of the colony's finest gold- and silversmiths, furniture and clock makers, and portrait painters. By 1760, the town was known as one of the most refined in the region.

Intellectual life was blooming, too. In 1727, William Parks of England printed the first issue of the *Maryland Gazette*, the colony's first newspaper. As the colony's official printer, Parks also published the colony's laws and the assembly's minutes, as well as political pamphlets, an almanac, and a schoolbook. Three years later, Parks moved to Virginia to found that colony's first newspaper.

Annapolis residents were able to browse through the town's bookstore, attend dances, and enjoy a night at the theater. In June 1752, a traveling company of actors used a warehouse to stage the first theatrical performance in the colony. Such performances became so popular that a brick theater was eventually built in Annapolis. George Washington attended the new theater's opening night in 1771.

Other, rougher types of entertainment also enlivened the residents of Annapolis. Men galloped through the fields and forests hunting foxes, played card games, and gambled. Perhaps the most popular pastime was horse racing. The first races in the colony were held at crossroads or outside taverns, where people of all classes wagered money on their favorite horse. These rough and unruly races were often the scene of *"Drunkeness, fighting, Hooping, hallowing [hollering], Swearing, Cursing, Wrestling."*

Spurred by their love of racing, some wealthy colonists began breeding their own racehorses. In 1745, Governor Samuel Ogle organized the first regulated horse race in the Colonies. Breeders from around the Chesapeake area traveled to Annapolis to take part in the race.

The home of Charles Carroll of Carrollton, pictured here with an African slave in front, still stands. It is the site of a museum and ongoing archaeological investigation into Maryland's colonial past.

THE GULF BETWEEN RICH AND POOR

Not everyone, however, was enjoying Maryland's golden age. During the mid-1700s, the number of poor people in the colony increased. Former indentured servants and convicts could not afford land in Maryland, especially in the 1760s when land prices rose. More and more people were forced to become tenant farmers, renting a plot of land to support themselves and their families.

Tenant farmers were often deeply in debt. Any person who owed money in the colony was legally forbidden to leave without a pass. Colonists who were unable to repay their debts faced a long stint in the town or county jail. The conditions of Maryland's jails were awful. In the 1730s, inmates of the Annapolis prison had to cut pieces of wooden beams from the ceiling to burn for warmth. Women were imprisoned alongside men. In 1736, a committee reported to the assembly: *"The Gaol of Annapolis besides being a place of Restraint and Confinement has also been a place of Death and Torments to Many Unfortunate People."*

Usually debtors were released from jail only when their families paid off their debt. Sometimes, prisoners petitioned the assembly for an early release. Those who were set free often had to agree to sell off all the goods they owned that were not needed in order to survive and earn a living.

In 1768, Maryland passed a law to build its first workhouses for the poor in five counties where poverty was a serious problem. Workhouses were places where poor people would be given housing in exchange for their labor. The same law appointed trustees in the counties who could make laws regarding the poor and punish *"such offenders as vagrants, beggars, and vagabonds."* The poor could be imprisoned in these new workhouses against their will for up to three months.

CHARLES COUNTY JUSTICE

A COMPLAINT WRITTEN BY A DEBTOR IMPRISONED IN THE
Charles County jail on November 5, 1768, illuminates the
terrible conditions in Maryland prisons. The debtor found

*the House not finished and leaky in the Roof and so open
that the Snow and Rain drove in . . . dropping down on
our Beds and the Floor covered with Ice and our Beds and
Bed Cloaths continually wet and frequently frozen Stiff
that I could have broke my Bed Cloaths like Ice, we wrote
to the Sheriff praying for Fire and let him know our
Condition the answer was let me hear no needless
Complaints. . . . Then the sheriff sent in a Kettle to make
a fire in but as there was no Chimney to vent the smoak but
a hole in the Door eight Inches wide and Twelve Inches deep
it is impossible to describe what we suffered with the Smoak
yet we were obliged to bear it or be froze to Death as some
of us were frost bit and all sick with a disorder in our Heads
and Eyes occasioned by the Smoak and hardship we had
suffered with wet and cold and continued in this deplorable
Condition till the 27th day of February 1769.*

The sheriff of the prison was fined by the assembly, but the
council refused to remove him from office.

With no voice in their colony's government, poor Maryland residents had little chance of improving their lives. With only wealthy or well-off colonists allowed to run for office, the poor were left with no representation in the colony's assembly. Property requirements or religious qualifications left only about one out of three white adult males able to vote.

BOUNDARY DISPUTES

During the mid-1700s, a long-standing feud between Maryland and Pennsylvania was finally laid to rest. The disagreement had started in 1681, when William Penn was granted land, which he called Pennsylvania, to the north of Maryland. Penn began building his new colony's capital, Philadelphia, on land that the first Lord Baltimore considered part of Maryland.

In the 1730s, the border dispute resulted in violence and bloodshed sometimes known as Cresap's War. In an attempt to strengthen his claim to the region, Lord Baltimore granted Maryland colonist Thomas Cresap 500 acres (203 ha) in present-day Wrightsville, Pennsylvania. Cresap built a home there and was prepared to defend it. He and his friends harassed, raided, and attacked German farmers in the region who refused to support Lord Baltimore's claim.

In 1736, a Pennsylvania sheriff arrested Cresap, now known as the "Maryland Monster," and took him to

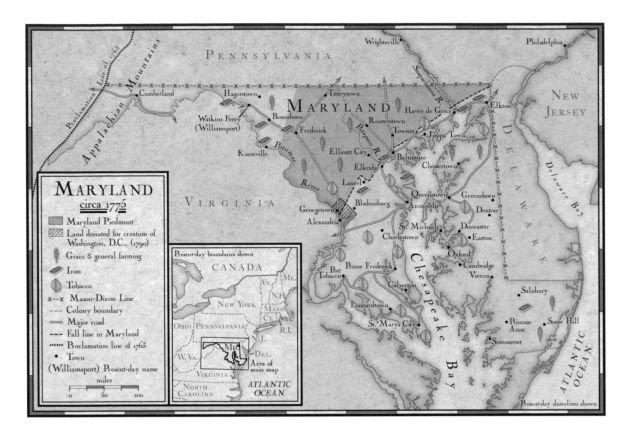

On the eve of the American Revolution, Maryland was a prosperous
mid-Atlantic colony. Its population of about 150,000 had replaced all but
a few hundred Native Americans. Tens of thousands were enslaved
Africans, most of whom worked planting and harvesting tobacco grown
on the Eastern and Western Shores of Chesapeake Bay. The demand for
grain led to a growth in settlement in the Piedmont region (dark green
area on the map) and the rise of cities such as Frederick and Baltimore,
which became a major shipping center. The colony's rich iron deposits also
spurred economic growth in the mid-1700s. In 1767, the boundary
dispute between Maryland and Pennsylvania was finally settled with the
acceptance of the Mason-Dixon Line. After the war, land for what would
become known as Washington, D.C. (see map), was donated by
Maryland. One of her native sons, a free black named Benjamin Banneker,
helped survey the site.

Philadelphia for trial. The following year, the king had him released and banned the granting of land in the contested area.

In 1760, both sides agreed to hire surveyors to set the exact coordinates of the boundaries between Maryland and Pennsylvania. Englishmen Charles Mason and Jeremiah Dixon began charting and mapping the region in 1763. They started 15 miles (24 km) south of Philadelphia, then headed west using the stars as guides. By 1767, the two had mapped out a line more than 230 miles (370 km) long. Mason and Dixon also measured out the boundary between Maryland and Delaware. Today, the boundary drawn by the two men is still known as the Mason-Dixon Line. In the coming years, the line would serve as the divider between North and South, free states and slave-owning states. ❧

Marking the MASON-DIXON LINE

As Mason and Dixon charted the boundary between Maryland and Pennsylvania, they left behind huge stone boulders at each mile to mark the border. Each square boulder was between 3.5 and 5 feet (1 and 1.5 m) long and weighed between 300 and 600 pounds (136 and 272 kg). Some have a carving of the Calvert coat of arms on one side and the Penn coat of arms on the other. Beginning in 1991, a group called the Mason and Dixon Line Preservation Partnership has tried to locate and document the stones before they are destroyed by time and human activity. Members of the group photograph and record the condition of each stone as they find it.

CHAPTER EIGHT

Seeking Self-Government

As problems between Great Britain and the American colonies heat up, Maryland colonists struggle to free themselves from Calvert control. During the Revolution, Maryland plays an important and historic role.

ince Maryland's earliest days, groups of colonists had wanted to shake off Calvert control. Now, colonists began wondering if they also needed to break free from Great Britain. In the mid-1700s, Parliament passed the first of a series of restrictive laws that affected Maryland's economy. The taxes were part of Britain's efforts to protect British trade and raise money to pay for the French and Indian War.

OPPOSITE: In this oil painting by Francis Blackwell Mayer, mariner and merchant Anthony Stewart sets fire to his own ship, the *Peggy Stewart*, at the insistence of Maryland colonists who opposed the British tax on the tea his ship brought into the Colonies.

TAXATION WITHOUT REPRESENTATION

The first act to affect Maryland was the Iron Act, passed in 1750. The law banned colonists from making the kinds of finished metal products that they imported from Britain, including tools and other hardware. It also prohibited colonists from building forges to make steel and from owning machines used for making finished iron goods. Although Britain relied on iron from Maryland and some of the other Colonies, it wanted to protect its craftsmen from American competition.

In the spring of 1765, Parliament enacted the Stamp Act. This new law placed a tax on all legal documents and printed materials, including newspapers and playing cards. Colonists were forced to buy stamps they then had to affix to these items. Maryland colonists were outraged.

In April, Jonas Green, editor of the *Maryland Gazette*, printed an article denouncing the tax. In the coming weeks, Green wrote more articles and letters opposing the tax, which was to take effect on November 1. The editor pledged to close down the paper if the act was not repealed.

Another major opponent of the Stamp Act was Daniel Dulany, Jr., the son of the founder of Frederick. In 1761, Dulany had been appointed to the council. Unlike other council members, however, he was sympathetic to the assembly. Governor Horatio Sharpe described Dulany as

Patriot—a colonist
who favored independ-
ence from England

*"fond of being thought a Patriot [favoring inde-
pendence from Britain] Councillor and rather
inclined to serve the People than the Propietary."*

The month before the Stamp Act went into effect,
Dulany wrote a pamphlet that became known as
"Considerations." In the pamphlet, he wrote that the 13
Colonies should not be taxed unless they had a representative in the British Parliament. Some modern historians
believe that Dulany's pamphlet was one of the most influ-
ential anti–Stamp Act protests in the Colonies.

Not all the protests against the act were so peaceful.
When colonists learned that an Annapolis merchant named
Zachariah Hood had accepted the job as the colony's stamp
officer, they organized a demonstration against him. Led by
a lawyer and assembly member named Samuel Chase, the
protesters hanged and burned a dummy made to look like
Hood. After the stamps arrived from London, the warehouse where they were stored mysteriously burned to the
ground. One visitor to Maryland during this time of turmoil noted that when the colonists talked about the
upcoming tax, *"Then was they Damning their souls if they would
pay and Damn them but they would fight to the last Drop of their blood
before they would Consent to such Slavery."*

Once the Stamp Act went into effect, some colonists
openly defied the law. Courts in Frederick issued documents without the required stamps. In February, Green
began publishing the *Gazette*—without stamps.

In early 1766, the first Sons of Liberty group in Maryland was formed in Baltimore. The group's formal title reflected its goals: Society for the Maintenance of Order and Protection of American Liberty. Before the group could take much action, news came from Britain that the hated Stamp Act had been repealed.

The late 1760s and early 1770s brought new laws that inflamed Maryland colonists. In 1767, for example, the Townshend Acts placed a series of taxes on goods imported into the 13 Colonies from Britain. These goods included glass, paint, and tea. In response, Baltimore residents proposed a plan to stop importing all goods from Britain. The boycott by Maryland and other Colonies eventually led to the repeal of most of the taxes.

BREAKING WITH THE PROPRIETOR

In 1771, Frederick Calvert, the sixth Lord Baltimore, died at the age of 40. Calvert named his son, 13-year-old Henry Harford, as his heir to the colony of Maryland.

After Calvert's death, open conflict between the court party and the country party erupted. The troubles began with an article published in the *Gazette*. The article supported the proprietor's right to control the colony and attacked members of the country party who opposed the proprietor and his representatives.

It wasn't long before the country party responded. Soon articles began appearing in the *Gazette* arguing that the colonists had the right to be free of all proprietary control. The articles were anonymous, but it was common knowledge that Charles Carroll, a prominent resident of Carrollton, was the author. Carroll spoke for many colonists in Maryland.

Charles Carroll of Carrollton, the only Catholic to sign the Declaration of Independence

As a result of Carroll's articles, a new party, known as the popular party, easily won the elections for the Maryland assembly in 1773. The assembly was now firmly in the hands of men who favored freedom from proprietary rule. In 1774, Carroll served as one of Maryland's delegates to the First Continental Congress in Philadelphia.

Continental Congress— America's governing body throughout the American Revolution

He was the only Roman Catholic to sign the Declaration of Independence in 1776.

In April 1774, Governor Robert Eden dismissed Maryland's colonial assembly for the last time. Two months later, delegates from the Maryland counties met at a special convention in Annapolis to form a new governing body. The Association of Maryland Freemen, as it became known, replaced the governor, council, and assembly.

BURNING THE *Peggy Stewart*

TEN MONTHS AFTER THE famous "tea party" in Boston, where Massachusetts colonists dumped tea into the harbor to protest taxes, colonists in Annapolis held their own event. In October 1774, they learned that the owner of the ship *Peggy Stewart* had brought 2,000 pounds (908 kg) of British tea into Maryland. Colonists who opposed the tea tax gathered at the docks. They forced the owner of the *Peggy Stewart* to set fire to his ship himself.

Not everyone applauded the violent event. Colonist John Galloway wrote that the burning *"makes all men of property reflect with horror on their present Situation to have their lives and propertys at the disposal & mercy of a Mob is Shocking indeed."*

In the coming years, the association would meet nine times. In July 1775, the group set aside proprietary rule. However, the delegates were still not sure whether they wanted to be independent from Britain.

THE REVOLUTION BEGINS

On April 19, 1775, battles between Patriots and British soldiers at Lexington and Concord in Massachusetts, marked the start of the American Revolution.

The Continental Congress requested that Maryland supply eight regiments of men. Counties quickly began organizing militia units. Wrote one Annapolis merchant, *"Every province is learning the life of arms. You may depend that we will die before we give up our liberties and have our property at the disposal of a damn lot of rascally ministers."*

At first, recruitment requirements were strict. Regulations warned, *"Enlist no man who is not able bodied, healthy, and a good marcher, nor such whose attachment to the liberties of America you have cause to suspect. . . ."* Volunteers who enlisted with the militia received payment plus the promise of land once the war was over. Eventually, because of shortages, the homeless, free blacks, and servants (with the consent of their masters) were allowed to join.

Maryland's militia earned what would become the state nickname, the Old Line State, because of its ability to stand firm and hold the line during the Battle of Long Island, in New York, in 1775. The battle was a disastrous defeat for the Americans, but Maryland soldiers stood strong and covered other Continental troops as they fled for safety. *"No regular troops ever made a more gallant resistance,"* wrote Tench Tilghman, a Maryland resident who served on General George Washington's staff. Maryland's militia served honorably, fighting for three years with Washington before heading south to the Carolinas to fight under General Nathanael Greene.

Maryland's militiamen, fighting under George Washington's command, were well armed and clothed during the winter months of 1775–1776.

TAKING A STAND

In June 1776, Sir Robert Eden, the last of Maryland's royal governors appointed by the king admitted defeat and left the colony for England. That same month, the Second Continental Congress met in Philadelphia. Maryland's delegates were reluctant to sign the Declaration of Independence, the document that declared the 13 Colonies to be independent of Britain. John Adams, a statesman who was among the first to push for independence, later wrote to Thomas Jefferson, the author of the Declaration, *"Neither the State of Maryland, nor of their delegates, were very early in their conviction of the necessity of independence, nor very forward in promoting it. . . . Maryland sent one, at least, of the most turbulent Tories that ever came to Congress."* Finally, Maryland's delegates received word from the Association of Maryland Freemen to vote for independence.

The First Printing

THE FIRST PRINTED, FULLY SIGNED COPY OF THE DECLARATION of Independence was published in January 1777 by Mary Katherine Goddard, from her print shop in Baltimore, Maryland. An earlier copy of the Declaration had been printed on July 4, but that document contained only two signatures, those of John Hancock and Charles Thomson. Goddard, who served as postmaster of Baltimore (likely the first woman to hold that position in America), was also responsible for distributing copies of the document throughout the 13 states.

Two months later, the association drafted Maryland's first constitution, a document that created a permanent state government. The constitution brought little real change for the poor citizens of Maryland. Control of the state government was left in the hands of those with land and money. The document did restore political rights for Catholics. Maryland's first elected governor, Thomas Johnson, took office in March 1777.

Although the former colony had now voted for freedom from British rule, many Marylanders remained loyal to Britain. These people were known as Loyalists, or Tories. Maryland even had a Tory regiment, the First Battalion of Maryland Loyalists, made up of Tories who had been driven out of Maryland at the start of the Revolution. At the end of the war, those still left in the regiment fled to Canada.

MARYLAND MAKES A DIFFERENCE

The colony of Maryland made important contributions to the war effort. Maryland's government required all households to donate half of their extra blankets to the soldiers in the Continental Army. The government later asked each family for one pair of shoes and white yarn stockings. Maryland also sent hay, tobacco, and food, including flour, beef, and grain to help feed the Patriot troops.

Continental Army—the troops who fought for American independence during the Revolution under the command of General George Washington

When the British threatened to take control of Philadelphia in late 1776, Maryland played host to the Continental Congress. Congressional delegates from the 13 former colonies met in Baltimore at the home of Jacob Fite.

Baltimore grew during the war. The town served as a supply center for the Continental Army, and Baltimore factories produced clothing, tools, and paper for the army. Baltimore shipyards built several ships that were used by the Continental Navy and by Maryland forces to defend the state from attack.

During the war, Baltimore was home to about 250 privateers. Privateers were ships that were authorized by the government to attack and rob British ships. Many of the privateers were funded by Maryland's wealthy merchants. Between 1776 and 1778, the privateers captured more than 500 British vessels.

privateer—a privately owned ship that is hired by a government to attack and rob the ships of enemy countries

Frederick also played an important role during the Revolution. The town was home to a powder storehouse and a factory that produced gun parts. The town was also the site of a camp for British and Hessian soldiers captured by the Continental Army and militia. The Hessians were German soldiers hired by the British to fight against the colonists.

Annapolis did its part, too, serving as a muster and shipping center. A hospital to treat wounded soldiers and a factory producing military leather goods were also set up

muster—the act of bringing troops together

in the city during the war. Annapolis continued to make history at the end of the American Revolution. On September 3, 1783, representatives of Britain and the United States signed the Treaty of Paris in Maryland's capital. The treaty formally ended the American Revolution. After the treaty was signed, Annapolis served as the temporary capital of the United States for about six months.

This painting shows General George Washington formally giving up his post as commander of the Continental Army to Congress in Annapolis, Maryland, the nation's temporary capital.

On April 28, 1788, Maryland lawmakers ratified, or approved, the U.S. Constitution, and Maryland became the seventh state. The state ceded land to the federal government for a new capital, which would be known as Washington, D.C. In the coming years, Maryland's location near the new capital and as a state sandwiched between North and South would put it in a precarious position in national conflicts.

TIME LINE

1524 Giovanni da Verrazano sails along Maryland's Eastern Shore, giving France a claim to the region.

1561 Pedro Menéndez de Avilés becomes the first European to explore Chesapeake Bay.

1588 Vicente Gonzales explores the bay up to its northernmost shoreline.

1603 English captain Bartholomew Gilbert is killed by Native Americans on Maryland's Eastern Shore.

1608 Virginia colonist John Smith explores the Chesapeake region.

1629 Lord Baltimore asks Charles I of England for land in Virginia.

1631 William Claiborne founds a trading post and settlement on Kent Island, off Maryland's Eastern Shore.

1632 Cecilius Calvert, the second Lord Baltimore, receives a grant of land in the northern section of Virginia Colony, which he names Maryland.

1633 The *Ark* and the *Dove* set sail for Maryland with more than 130 settlers on board.

1634 St. Marys City is founded on the Western Shore.

1635 Colonial forces take control of Kent Island from William Claiborne.

1645 During Ingle's Rebellion, Richard Ingles and a group of followers take control of St. Marys City. Calvert forces retake the city a year later.

1649 Maryland passes the Toleration Act, mandating religious freedom.

1654 Puritans take control of Maryland's government and repeal the Toleration Act.

1655 Governor Stone's forces are defeated at the Battle of the Severn.

1657 Lord Baltimore signs a peace treaty with Richard Bennett and William Claiborne.

1660 Maryland colonists declare war on the Iroquois.

1675 Governor Charles Calvert becomes the third Lord Baltimore upon the death of his father, Cecilius Calvert.

1688 James II, the last Catholic monarch of England, is dethroned during the Glorious Revolution.

1689 During Coode's Rebellion, Protestant John Coode and the Associators take control of St. Marys City and overthrow proprietary rule.

1692 Maryland becomes a royal colony. The first royal governor arrives in Maryland.

1695 The first mass shipment of slaves is brought into Maryland.

1715 Benedict Leonard, the fourth Lord Baltimore, is awarded proprietary rights to Maryland.

1717 Britian begins transporting convicts to work in Maryland.

1727 The colony's first newspaper—the *Maryland Gazette*—starts publication.

1729 Baltimore is incorporated.

1739 Slaves in Prince George's County plot an unsuccessful rebellion.

1745 Daniel Dulany founds Frederick.

1750 Great Britain passes the Iron Act.

1752 A troupe of traveling actors puts on the colony's first theatrical performance.

1760 Lord Baltimore and William Penn agree to hire surveyors to decide the border between the two colonies.

1765 British Parliament passes the Stamp Act.

1766 Maryland's first Sons of Liberty group is formed.

1767 Charles Mason and Jeremiah Dixon finish measuring the boundary between Maryland and Pennsylvania, a border called the Mason-Dixon Line.

1771 Frederick Calvert, sixth Lord Baltimore, dies, naming his illegitimate 13-year-old son his heir.

1774 The *Peggy Stewart*, a ship carrying tea from Great Britain, is burned.

1775 Battles at Lexington and Concord, in Massachusetts, mark the start of the American Revolution. Maryland sets aside proprietary rule.

1777 Maryland's first elected governor takes office.

1783 The Treaty of Paris is signed in Annapolis, officially ending the Revolution. The town serves as temporary capital of the new nation.

1788 Maryland becomes the seventh U.S. state on April 28, when lawmakers ratify the Constitution.

Resources

BOOKS

Brugger, Robert J. *Maryland, A Middle Temperament: 1634–1980.* Baltimore, MD: The Johns Hopkins University Press, 1996.

Earle, Alice Morse. *Child Life in Colonial Days.* Whitefish, MT: Kessinger, 2004.

Gray, Edward G. *Colonial America: A History in Documents.* New York: Oxford University Press, 2002.

Miller, Brandon Marie. *Declaring Independence: Life During the American Revolution.* Minneapolis, MN: Lerner, 2005.

Nobleman, Marc Tyler. *Colonial America: History Pockets.* Monterey, CA: Evan-Moor, 2003.

Wood, Peter H. *Strange New Land: Africans in Colonial America.* New York: Oxford University Press, 2003.

WEB SITES

Catoctin Mountain Park
http://www.nps.gov/cato/index.htm
Home page of the National Park Service's Catoctin Mountain Web site, with historical information on the iron industry in Maryland.

Exploring Maryland's Roots
http://mdroots.thinkport.org/
A Web site from Maryland Public Television with all kinds of fascinating historical information about the colony.

Historic St. Marys City
http://www.stmaryscity.org/
Information about one of Maryland's first settlements.

Maryland Online Encyclopedia
http://www.mdoe.org/
An online encyclopedia with information on many aspects of Maryland history.

Maryland State Archives Museum Online
http://www.msa.md.gov/msa/educ/exhibits/html/exhibit.html
Instant access to documents that were important to Maryland's founding.

The National Archives Experience
http://www.archives.gov/national-archives-experience/charters/constitution_founding_fathers_maryland.html
Brief biographies of the nation's founders from Maryland

QUOTE SOURCES

CHAPTER ONE

p. 19 "so thicke with...catch fish with." Quinn, David B. *Early Maryland in a Wider World*. Detroit: Wayne State University Press, 1982. p.280; p. 20 "All the Country...with trees." Land, Aubrey C. *Colonial Maryland, A History*. Millwood, NY: KTO Press, 1981, p.18.

CHAPTER TWO

p. 26 "cause all Acts...as may be." Land, Aubrey C. *Colonial Maryland, A History*. Millwood, NY: KTO Press, 1981. p. 7; "this amazed...Stoutest hearts." http://www.msa.md.gov/msa/speccol/sc2200/sc2221/000017/000005/pdf/pp29-31.pdf; p. 27 "wanted noething... our ruine," Brugger, Robert J. *Maryland, A Middle Temperament: 1634–1980*. Baltimore, Maryland: The Johns Hopkins University Press, 1996, p. 8; "We will use...common with us." http://facstaff.unca.edu/epearson/father_white.htm; p. 32 "We do disassent...to be void." Brugger, p. 13.

CHAPTER THREE

p. 38 "contrived so...pritty and convenient." http://wps.prenhall.com/wps/media/objects/171/175116/05_leah.HTM; "The dwellings are... them everywhere." Brugger, Robert J. *Maryland, A Middle Temperament: 1634–1980*. Baltimore, Maryland: The Johns Hopkins University Press, 1996, p. 25; "more favorable...family life." Horn, James. *Adapting to the New World*. Chapel Hill, North Carolina: The University of North Carolina Press, 1996, p. 230; p. 39 "The cold...sharp." Land, Aubrey C. *Colonial Maryland, A History*. Millwood, NY: KTO Press, 1981. p. 20; p. 40 "A fiery Pulse...of a Physician." http://www.mith2.umd.edu/eada/html/display.php?docs=cooke_sotweed.xml&action=show; "Meat, Drinke,...other necessaries." Brugger, p. 16; p. 42 "The labour servants...good exercises." Horn, p. 266; "[They have] maize...as well as themselves." Horn, p. 275.

CHAPTER FOUR

p. 48 "The King...King," Land, Aubrey C. *Colonial Maryland, A History*. Millwood, NY: KTO Press, 1981. p. 46; p. 50 "As for Mistress...against her." Meyers, Debra. *Common Whores, Vertuous Women, and Loveing Wives*. Bloomington, IN: Indiana University Press, 2003. p.25; p. 52 "bee any wais...or her consent." Land, p. 50; p. 54 "forbear disturbing... authority from you." http://djs.state.md.us/megafile/msa/speccol/sc2900/sc2908/000001/000003/html/am3p-10.html.

CHAPTER FIVE

p. 63 "wholly ruine...the [majority]...." http://www.msa.md.gov/megafile/msa/speccol/sc2900/sc2908/000001/000005/html/am5-17.html; p. 64 "The province of...house of iniquity." Scharf, Thomas J. *History of Maryland, Volume 1*. Hatboro, PA: Tradition Press, 1967, p.282; "Maryland is now...in pieces." Brugger, p. 37.

CHAPTER SIX

p. 70 "wicked Lewd and...drunkenness, Swearing,...whatsoever" http://www.msa.md.gov/megafile/msa/speccol/sc2900/sc2908/000001/000005/html/am5-17.html; pp. 71–72 "There are in...dais in the week." Land, Aubrey C. *Colonial Maryland, A History*. Millwood, NY: KTO Press, 1981. p. 96; p. 74 "frequent assembly" http://djs.state.md.us/megafile/msa/speccol1/sc2900/sc2908/000001/000061.html; p. 75 "A new Negro,...can be conquer'd." Brugger, Robert J. *Maryland, A Middle Temperament: 1634–1980*. Baltimore, Maryland: The Johns Hopkins University Press, 1996, p. 62; p. 76 "Living in foreign...Death at Home." Brugger, p. 87.

CHAPTER SEVEN

p. 86 "Drunkeness, fighting,... Wrestling." Brugger, Robert J. *Maryland, A Middle Temperament: 1634–1980*. Baltimore, Maryland: The Johns Hopkins University Press, 1996, p. 73; p. 87 "The Gaol of...Unfortunate People." Brugger, p. 100; p. 87 "such offenders...and vagabonds." http://djs.state.md.us/megafile/msa/speccol/sc2900/sc2908/000001/000061/html/am61p-96.html; p. 88 "the House not...February 1769." http://www.msa.md.gov/megafile/msa/speccol/sc2900/sc2908/000001/000032/html/am32-337.html.

CHAPTER EIGHT

p. 95 "fond of...than the Propietary." Land, Aubrey C. *Colonial Maryland, A History*. Millwood, NY: KTO Press, 1981. p. 245; "Then was they...such Slavery." Brugger, Robert J. *Maryland, A Middle Temperament: 1634–1980*. Baltimore, Maryland: The Johns Hopkins University Press, 1996, p. 104; p. 98 "makes all men...Shocking indeed." Brugger, p. 113; "Every province...rascally ministers." Brugger, p. 116; p. 99 "Enlist no man...to suspect...." http://www.msa.md.gov/megafile/msa/speccol/sc2900/sc2908/000001/000078/html/am78-94.html; "No regular troops...resistance." http://memory.loc.gov/cgi-bin/query/r?ammem/lhbcb:@field(DOCID+@lit(lhbcb22944div2)) http://www.msa.md.gov/megafile/msa/speccol/sc2900/sc2908/000001/000082/html/am82b-393.html; p. 100 "Neither the State...came to Congress." Bergh, Albert Ellery (editor). *The Writings of Thomas Jefferson, Vol. 15*. Washington, D.C.: Thomas Jefferson Memorial Association of the United States, 1903. p.337.

INDEX

ABOUT THE AUTHOR AND CONSULTANT

ROBIN DOAK is a writer of fiction and nonfiction books for children, ranging from elementary to high school levels. Subjects she has written about include American immigration, the 50 states, American presidents, and U.S. geography. Doak is a former editor of *Weekly Reader* and has also written numerous support guides for educators. She holds a Bachelor of Arts degree in English, with an emphasis on journalism, from the University of Connecticut and lives near her alma mater in Portland. She is also the author of *Voices from Colonial America: New Jersey, Georgia, California,* and *South Carolina.*

JAMES D. RICE is an Associate Professor of History at the State University of New York at Plattsburgh. He earned his Ph.D. from the University of Maryland, College Park. Rice's publications focus on crime and punishment in early Maryland, on community life in early western Maryland, and on Native Americans in the Chesapeake Bay region. He lives in the Adirondack Mountains of New York.

ILLUSTRATION CREDITS

1685

ARCTIC

BAFFINS BAY

NEW NORTH WALES

NEW SOUTH WALES

HUDS

Tract of Land full of Wild Bulls

NEW MEXICO

New Mexico

SEA OF CALIFORNIA

NEW ALBION

NewBiscaia

ZACATECAS

THE GOLF or BAY OF MEXICO

SEA

OF

NEW SPAIN